BREAKING ORBIT

HOW TO WRITE, PUBLISH AND LAUNCH YOUR
FIRST BESTSELLER ON AMAZON WITHOUT A
MAILING LIST, BLOG OR SOCIAL MEDIA
FOLLOWING

JONATHAN GREEN

DRAGON GOD BOOKS

CONTENTS

1

THE FORCE OF GRAVITY

"Sorry, your agent has decided he doesn't want to meet with you after all."

I flew from Nashville to New York and booked a hotel I could barely afford just to meet this literary agent, a friend of my father. They had done a lot of business in the past, and he was supposed to be my entry into the glorious world of the professional author.

I wasted time, money, energy and hope.

I was walking down the lonely streets of New York City, wondering why the agent stopped returning my calls the day before our meeting. And then I got this brush-off email from some assistant who I had never spoken to in the past.

I felt like the city that never sleeps kicked me right between the sticks.

Nobody around me knew what I was experiencing, but I felt like they did. I was humiliated. To have someone look at the totality of your existence and judge you lacking is brutal, cruel and mean. For a moment, I considered never writing another word.

Maybe I should go back to teaching or look for another job. But that wasn't a realistic option. When you get fired from one of the top twenty universities in the country you can't go back. I was over teaching. I didn't want to slave away at the front of a classroom ever again. I wanted to move forward with my life.

I was such a terrible author that my agent didn't even reject me personally. He dumped me like a cowardly teenager. The cold shoulder. The brush-off. He could have told me before I spent money I didn't have on plane tickets and hotels and overpriced big city food. Part of me wanted to just lie down on the sidewalk and cry forever.

My next book grossed over five million dollars in sales. The very book that this agent rejected became one of my greatest successes. It still sells every single day all these years later.

This book is the story of how I turned rejection into thirty bestsellers and a life on one of the greatest tropical beaches in the world.

I took that kick in the pants so you don't have to. You don't have to deal with rejection letters from agents and publishers: the New York elite. You can write and publish Kindle books fast. You can replace your income, pay your bills and create an amazing life.

By the end of this book, you will have all the tools and knowledge that you need.

You Should Get in the Game

Most people don't think they are great writers. They find it hard to imagine that they would ever write or publish words that other people want to read.

It's amazing to think that twenty-four hours a day, someone in the world is reading words that I wrote. This magical feeling is how we can attain immortality. As long as people read your books, you can live forever.

I'm not a very talented writer. People occasionally feel the need to send me letters to remind me that I'm no Hemingway. During his life, he only published seven novels. He published some collections of short stories and non-fiction, but he's not remembered for those. Only seven novels and he attained a level of immortality. If I wrote at the same pace, I would only have two books under my belt by now instead of more than one hundred.

The most financially successful author in the world is James Patterson. Make no mistake: he outsells everyone else. Every year another one of his books becomes a movie. He is the most prolific author going, constantly writing new novels and working with new partners. Quantity is a quality all on its own.

The secret to my success is speed. When you write and publish books fast, you can grow a real business. Writing books for glory and acclaim is not the path I teach. Becoming an Amazon author is about generating income. The only statistic to look at each month is your revenue. Whether you sell one book or ten thousand is irrelevant.

The Kindle program is fantastic because it puts you in total control of your destiny. You will make more money selling your book for $2.99 than you would selling it for $14.99 through a publisher. When you work with a publisher, you lose much of your voice. Sure, they help you with editing, but they also decide the cover and control the entire marketing strategy.

My last book, Serve No Master, was the story of my entire journey from fired university professor to living my dreams on a tropical island. The moment I took control of my destiny, everything changed.

Together we are about to go on an incredible journey. When you take control of your destiny, the world turns from a frightening nightmare into a wondrous opportunity. You no longer wonder if people will like your next book or if you will have enough money to make rent. Those worries will fade away.

The system in this book is about building a business. You are going to write and release books that people love to read and share with their friends. When your system is in place, you will develop passive income streams. My books are my children's inheritance. If something horrible happened to me today, they would continue to receive royalty checks for years.

Most of us have no plan for retirement, and our kids will be lucky if they have enough inheritance to pay for the funeral. That is about to change. Building a Kindle empire creates revenue that grows while you sleep, while you travel, and even long after you're gone. This is the type of business that you can leave to your children and know they are protected.

Why You Should Listen to Me

I could load up this chapter with pictures of royalty checks or pictures of all my bestseller stars. Maybe I could fill it with pictures of me driving expensive cars or flying around in private jets. But that's not what you're here for.

You already bought this book, so I know you're a believer. You want to achieve your dreams and grow something amazing.

I currently live on a beautiful tropical island. It's considered to be one of the top surfing spots in the world. Sometimes it is fourth on the list, and sometimes it's eighth. The ranking is always fluctuating on those lists, but for me it's perfect. I have loads of pictures on my website of my little slice of paradise if you want to see them.

I live with my girlfriend just fifty meters from the water with nothing in the way except a pool and a little grass. We have two amazing children, and life is close to perfect. I haven't worn a long-sleeve shirt in years, let alone a jacket. Every day here is warm; that's the beauty of the tropics.

If I so desire, I can save this document and walk outside, catching world-class waves within ten minutes. My family and I live in our personal definition of paradise.

Writing pays for every single aspect of my life. My words pay for the food my children eat, the house they live in and the clothes they wear. I don't have a separate day job. My writing employs more than six people full-time. I pump money into the local economy with the revenue from my words.

There are plenty of books out there about writing. Maybe you've read some of them. I don't make a living teaching people how to be writers; I earn a living directly from my writing. Do you want to learn how to start a business from a teacher or someone running a real business?

What You Will Learn

This book is about more than just writing and publishing a book. It's about more than my system that turns every book I write into a best-seller. That's just the tip of the iceberg, and you deserve so much more.

By the end of this little journey together, you will be able to write books that stay on the bestseller list for years. Your books will be the foundation of a business that supports your family. Most people see a book as an event, a moment in time.

A single book can make you a lot of money, but one day it can all disappear; people stop reading books all the time. Your new business will be shockproof. Rather than depend on the revenue from a single, lucky book to pay your bills, you will construct an entire business.

A business is something that can last; something that you can pass on to your children. Writing a book and launching it is just phase one. Building a connection with your readers that turns into more book sales, more product sales and a lasting relationship is the key.

You are going to learn how to:

- Choose your first topic to write about
- Find an audience desperate to read your book
- Launch a book with reviews and traffic
- Maintain momentum with your book for years
- Turn your book into a following that you can reach every single day
- Generate ten times more revenue from your books outside of Amazon

FREE GIFT

I have a special gift for you. You've finished reading the introduction, so you know a little bit about me. This book focuses on launching books in digital and paperback format. That's just part of the game. Releasing audio books can increase your passive income by 30%.

Just click this link to get my entire audiobook training course. I will walk you through the entire process.

CLICK HERE TO BOOST YOUR INCOME BY 30%

FREE GIFT

ServeNoMaster.com/audio

2

A SIMPLE PLAN

Before we build our plan, we need to know our destination. People write books for many different reasons, and each of them requires a different strategy.

There are two main reasons people read this book: they have a story they want to tell, or they want to make money from books.

You may have a passion for telling your story. Many people who write fiction fall into this category. Perhaps you have helped people with your work for so long that you want to spread the message to a larger audience.

The story drives these types of books. You begin with the message, and then you seek out the audience. Ninety-nine percent of authors follow this approach. They write a book and throw it into the world without doing any research. Their sales will depend on hope and luck.

When the project or the topic itself drives you, the book becomes the end result. Your primary goal is to release that story into the world.

The second type of writer wants to build a business. This person sees writing as a step on the path to their goals. They want to create books that serve a purpose. They want to release books that make money.

People in the second camp start with market research. They look for the audience, find out what that audience wants, and then give it to them. They still write about topics that interest them, but they factor the audience into their decisions.

If you have a story you want to tell and don't care whether the audience exists, then my ability to help you will be limited. Following the process in this book will get your book out into the world. You will get a lot of eyeballs on your book. Like warfare, however, the book business is a democracy and the readers get a vote.

Desiring to help people is very admirable, but if you create a book that appeals to a very small group of people you won't sell very many units.

We will start our book creation journey with research. The better your research at the beginning of your process, the more profitable you will be at the end of your process.

If passion totally drives you, I can still help you. We will put together a great book and get a lot of people reading it. Just know in advance that you can't create an audience out of nothing. You can write the greatest book in the world about customizing pagers, but if the audience isn't there the book won't sell.

(In case you're younger than me, a pager or beeper was a small electronic device that existed before the cell phone. People could call your pager and leave their phone number and nothing else. You then had to find the nearest payphone to call them. Writing a book about pagers would fail because nobody uses them anymore.)

The start to your passion project should still be research. Find the closest audience to your message and design a book that will appeal to them.

I Love Geometry

Breaking Orbit is the second book under the Serve No Master brand. Many of my books in the past have been under pen names to fit their markets better. I have already blocked out and planned ten different topics that I will write about over the next year.

Whether you are writing fiction or non-fiction, you need a series of books to be profitable.

The average self-published book on Amazon sells for $2.99. With a seventy-percent commission, you make just around two bucks per sale.

If you create one book on your topic, each new customer is worth two dollars. After they buy your book, there is nothing else for them and they move on to the next author. Your entire business depends on continually finding new readers.

When you create a series or a collection of related books, something very magical happens. The majority of your readers will buy multiple books, and many will read through your entire series.

I love to read science-fiction. When I find a new author, I read through all of their books voraciously. Some authors have one book, and when I finish reading it I am hungry for more content, but there is nothing left for me. I have to find another new author.

I read some authors who have more than twenty books in their series. I read that entire series and follow these incredible, epic adventures. I will stay there through the entire journey even if the books are only average. I will stick with less than stellar books because I am hooked on the ride. Having a longer series can make up for targeting a limited audience.

The first author makes two dollars when I discover their work, but the second one will make ten times more money. With a fiction series, you don't have to invent new worlds and characters constantly; you can continue in the universe you have already built.

Americans are voracious for extended stories. So many television shows have more than two hundred episodes because we enjoy serial stories. We love developing a connection with our favorite characters.

I am primarily a non-fiction author. When I create a book, I always think about creating a series of related books. Creating a one-off book on an isolated topic is a high-risk strategy. If I create ten books on similar topics, I only need ONE to be a hit. People will read that one and then read the rest of the books in that collection. I am no longer risking everything on a single book. I can control the odds of financial success.

The more books you add to your series the greater your income. The graph of this geometric growth is a parabola. Each month your income will grow, and the graph of your profits will look like a rocket ship blasting out to space. You will more than double your income every time you add new books to your series.

If you are driven by passion first, then creating a series is especially important. You can turn a limited readership into a profitable business simply by offering each reader more content to purchase from you.

I love reading supernatural detective stories. Right now this is a very limited niche with less than ten authors on Amazon. Most people would look at that space and avoid it because there just isn't enough meat on the bone. But the authors in that space sell a lot of books. I will read every book in one of those series simply because there is no alternative.

Some of the books that I read, I don't like very much. I don't enjoy how the author writes, or the main characters are unpleasant, but I keep reading because I am locked into the series.

No matter your topic, goals or passion, creating a series of books is the foundation of financial success. Planning multiple books is the first step in the path to building your literary empire.

3

FINDING YOUR NICHE

Y ou can write a book that you want to write and hope to find an audience, or you can make money, but you have to choose right now.

I work with a lot of coaching students and personally help them build their book strategy. Often they come to me with a superb idea but no research. They have a brilliant idea but no idea if anyone wants it.

Inventors make the same mistake when they create a solution for a problem that doesn't exist.

When I was in high school, someone invented a very expensive radar system to help you park in your garage. It would beep if you were too close to the wall. There is a low-tech alternative solution to this problem.

Park your car correctly once and then hang a tennis ball on a string touching your windshield. Every time you park your car, drive until you hit the tennis ball and then stop. You can park without annoying beeping driving you crazy or spending hundreds of dollars on this invention.

You might have a brilliant idea, but if the audience doesn't exist, nothing matters. You can write the greatest book in the world, but if nobody reads it, your message is lost.

I know it feels like I've been talking about this for ages, but this foundational lesson is critical to your long-term success. The way you start your journey will determine the ending. I want you to achieve massive financial success, write a bestseller, quit your job and then leave me a glowing review for this book. Unfortunately, to get you there I have to start with a little tough love.

At the beginning of this book, I offered you a free gift. I created additional training on converting your book into audiobook format. You just fill in your email address, and I send you the bonus material instantly.

If you aren't sure about your topic and want a little feedback, just reply to that email. It goes directly to me, not an assistant halfway around the world. I'll take a peek and help guide you down the path. I want you to succeed, and I'm happy to help guide you to your audience. You are not alone on this journey. This book is not a one-way conversation; if you talk to me, I will help you.

Amazon Search

The start of any project is research. The first place I like to research is on Amazon itself. There are some very particular tools that I use to help me with my research, but first I want to show you how to find your audience without spending a penny.

On Amazon, search for your topic inside the Kindle category. Just type "space marines" or "tinnitus" into the search box. We only want to search Kindle, because the data is better than looking at the entire books category.

Amazon tracks everything you do when you read a digital book. Amazon right now knows you are reading this page in my book. They know how fast you read, what time of day you read, and your favorite subjects.

Amazon gathers digital data in real-time. With physical books, Amazon only knows if you made the purchase. There is no data on your reading habits. If you are reading the paperback version of this book, then Amazon has no idea if you read the book or not.

Look at the ten most popular books on your potential topic. If Amazon ranks a book in the top 30,000, then it is a winner. I want to find five books in this range to ensure that it's something people are interested in. When Amazon ranks a book in the top 30,000, I know that it's making at least $100 a month on its own. That might not sound like a lot, but when you have twenty books in your series, it turns into a nice passive income stream.

Only your Kindle sales affect this number. Later on, I will show you how to multiply this revenue with physical sales, sales directly from your website, and affiliate sales.

I don't want to get into a market where there isn't enough money to go around. I performed the tinnitus search yesterday and noticed that the top book is selling one or two copies a week. Do I want to make ten bucks a month from a book? Not really.

Topics that are huge in other markets sometimes have no traction on Amazon. There are no great books on teaching kids to swim on Amazon. It's an important topic, and as a father it's close to my heart. I taught my daughter to swim, and I'm currently teaching my son. When I wanted to improve as a teacher, I went to Amazon first; I was curious to see if there was a market.

If you think for just a moment, you will not be surprised that this is a limited market. This niche is limited to parents who have children and a pool. Or parents with young children near a lake, river or ocean. The number of people who meet these conditions limits the size of the niche.

The second limitation is the format. Can you really teach a kid to swim from a book? Most people prefer using video for this type of training. You would do much better creating a swim-training DVD. That would sell a lot more than a book.

When you begin to analyze the top books under your keyword, you will notice their category ranks. If there is a category that closely matches your idea, you want to go to that category page. In my tinnitus research, I found that there are two highly relevant categories. There is a Kindle category just for hearing problems, and another one for audiology and speech pathology.

When I go to the audiology category, I notice that the books are very expensive. The top book is over $115. Audiology must be a textbook category. We have found an interesting category if you are a professional who wants to create a textbook. For most people, this category is not a good fit. Writing textbooks is a long and arduous project. That top book is over four hundred pages long, and filled with research and footnotes.

Additionally, none of the top books are about tinnitus. They are mostly about larger speech and communication issues. This category isn't a good fit for my initial idea.

The hearing problems category is a much better fit for this concept. Several of the top books in this category are about tinnitus, so I know I'm now in the right place. Scrolling through, I notice that there are romance novels and nursing exam training books in here. When I see books that clearly don't belong in a category, I know that someone is trying to manipulate Amazon to get a bestseller star. Inappropriate books invading a category is a red flag and the sign of a weak category. The best-selling books in the hearing problems category aren't even related to the topic.

The top book in the entire category is ranked 37,127 on Amazon today. According to my tool, that book is making $54 a month, and I think that figure might be a little generous. Do I want to dominate a category where my best case scenario is ten bucks a week? I would have to write one hundred books at that level to generate a decent living.

When you find a topic, keyword or category where several books are in the top 30,000 on Amazon, you have a winner. When you don't, you have a loser.

Clickbank

Amazon is just the beginning of my research process. I want to know how the wider world views the topic as well. We must find out if this topic is popular and profitable in the direct response world.

Before I write a book, I think about building a business. I want to sell additional products, services and training to my customers. I want to meet all of their needs. One of the great ways to expand your offerings is to find more expensive, but related, products to promote. Getting paid to recommend products is called affiliate marketing, and I'll go into greater detail later in the book in the section on building a list, but for now I just want to see if there is a secondary market.

My preferred secondary market is called Clickbank. I can go through their marketplace to see if there are products related to my potential topics. There are statistics on pricing, how well the offer sells, and my potential commissions if I recommend a product. This information gives me a feel for the DEPTH of a market. Depth is critical when building a business.

For some markets, people buy a single product to fix a single problem and then they disappear. They never ask the author for help again. One of the greatest examples of this is in the dating and relationship space. The majority of the books for men are about starting a relationship. How to meet a woman, say hello and start a relationship.

The books for women are about relationship maintenance and growth. There are books on dating, engagement, marriage, kids and more.

If you sell a man a book and solve his problem, you will never see him ever again. He buys your book, learns how to meet women, finds a great girlfriend and forgets you ever existed. You fixed his problem, but now the relationship is over.

When you sell a relationship book to a woman, however, she takes the long view. Men view relationships as an event, but women view them as a journey. For this reason, you can sell a woman products that help her throughout the course of the relationship. Relationship advice for women is a great market because there is great depth.

When I'm looking at Clickbank, I want to see more than just

depth of market. I also want to see the sales pages for similar products. If you have a book about dog training, take a look at the most
popular dog training courses. What promises do they make on the
sales page? What problems do they fix? What information does this
course include?

I will use the answers to these questions in my book and on my
Amazon listing page. This information is gold that most people
ignore. If a promise can sell a fifty-dollar book, it can certainly sell a
three-dollar one.

Udemy

Udemy is another platform that is growing right now. This platform
only sells video courses. They have a little affiliate program, but I'm
more interested in their data.

Search for your topic and look at the top listings. Most courses on
Udemy are now between ten and twenty dollars, which is closer to
the price point of your potential book.

The number of people who purchased each course, the sales
message, the number of reviews, the content of every single review
and the course table of contents are all listed on the course page. If
nobody is buying the course or the reviews are bad, that is a red flag.

When you find a course with good traction and reviews, you
know that your topic has legs. Your new market has secondary products at low and medium price points. Therefore this is a market
where you can build an entire business. Save the links to any courses
that fit your criteria to use later in the second research phase.

Google

Next, you want to expand your search beyond specific marketplaces.
Instead of just looking at products and sales channels, it's time to find
where your audience lives. Search your key terms in multiple search
engines to get a wider perspective of the types of websites that rise to
the top.

You are looking for blogs, forums, and websites that are specifically about your space. A forum about hearing is good, but a forum about tinnitus is even better. Once you find a few sites that are close to your topic, check their rankings in Alexa. This tool tracks the popularity of websites and ranks them. You are looking to see how much traction a topic has. If the most popular blog in the world has no traffic, that is a big red flag. If the forum has no traffic and very few posts, that is another red flag.

Take the time to look at what people in your new audience are discussing. The most popular blog posts and forum topics reveal what your audience worries about the most. Save the links to these sites; you are going to use them again in the book creation process.

Forums are an invaluable resource. People ask the very questions that your book needs to answer. Your audience tells you exactly what they need to hear before you write the first word. The more you understand your audience, the easier it is to satisfy them.

This research applies to fiction as much as non-fiction. Readers in forums share what they like and don't like about every book they read. It's so helpful to get a review before you write your book. You can avoid pitfalls that you didn't even know were there!

Inventing the Wheel

Being the first person with a new idea is exciting. When I have an idea that nobody else is pursuing, my first thought is that I'm a genius, and I thought of something before anyone else. But just maybe it's an idea with no competition because nobody cares about it.

I have no interest in re-inventing the wheel; I would rather improve it. I was talking to someone on my team yesterday, who was shocked that I would put out a book in a market with competition. That's what I want. I want to be in a space that I know is working.

I am completely aware that there are other books on Amazon about how to publish books on Amazon. There are probably hundreds of them by now. That tells me it's a good topic. A few people are doing really well, and many others that aren't selling anything.

I performed deep research, as I will show you later in this book. As long as my book is high quality and works, there is room in the market for me. This guide is the exact process I have used to become a bestseller over thirty times in a row. I have taught it to other clients and students in the past. I know that my system works. I know that if you take action, you will achieve the success you desire.

People are always reading more books. I have read hundreds of books on space marines, and I will probably read thousands more in my lifetime. The market is not finite. Don't worry about competition. Focus on creating the best product you can and you will rise to the top in your space.

4

TOOLS OF THE TRADE - RESEARCH

I am an affiliate for some of the products and services that I will mention in this book. They pay me a percentage of each sale as a thank-you for recommending them if you use my link. You are free to do a Google search for each tool to bypass my commission if you so choose.

With each tool, I will show you a free alternative first. I have already taught you how to research a topic without spending a penny, but now I'm going to show you the tools that I use to speed up that process.

There is not a single tool or technique in this book that I don't use for my projects. Everything in this book is something that I have used in the last seven days, and usually in the past 24 hours. Don't feel obligated to use any of my links, but if you choose to, I greatly appreciate it. When you are building your business, much of your income will be generated by similar links. You will want your audience to click them. Using my links is an excellent way to build up some great karma. ;)

KDP Rocket

KDP Rocket is a new tool, and it's pretty secret. I checked the sales stats, and I think less than fifty people in the world are using it. One of my students pointed this tool out to me, and I appreciate that. KDP Rocket works as a standalone search tool.

Enter your search term and the software generates unique variations, as well as Google traffic, Amazon traffic, and some profitability calculations. This software is hands-down the best Amazon keyword tool on the market. Every other tool only uses the Amazon suggestion box. This tool will generate three or four times more keywords that you didn't even consider.

The tool can quickly tell me if a market or keyword has any traction. When I find some keywords or topics that give me a good feeling, I want to dig into Amazon more deeply.

The one danger with using tools or doing quick research is false positives, which can happen when searching manually as well.

A false positive is where you enter a keyword, and only the top book is making a killing. This outlier will throw off all of your averages. KDP Rocket looks at the top twenty results of a search, estimates the total revenue of all twenty books combined and then divides that number by twenty. What you have there is the average income from a book in the top twenty.

Normally this method is fine, but if the top book is making ten grand a month and the next nineteen are making zero, the software will tell you that the average profit for the keyword is $500 a month. While technically accurate, this information doesn't help when you create a book that is #2 in the keyword and makes three dollars a month.

The second false positive is a dead keyword. No matter what term you type into Amazon, it will generate results. It never says "nothing here." Sometimes I come up with a keyword that has loads of sales, but when I dig deeper, I learn that nobody actually uses that term. It's just similar to a real term.

With KDP Rocket, you can click on "analyze" to see a detailed breakdown of the top twenty books. It's all housed within the external tool so that you can scan stats very quickly. You can quickly check to see if all of the books are making money or if there is just one outlier messing up the curve.

I wholeheartedly recommend using KDP Rocket as your starting point; it's one of the most powerful tools in your research arsenal. No other tool or manual technique generates as many unique keywords.

KDspy

I have been using KDSpy for a very long time now. This tool is a browser plugin. When I run a search within Amazon, I can click on this tool to get data faster. It shows me each book's ranking, price and other stats without me having to look at each book's listing page manually. This tool saves me time.

Originally, I used spreadsheets to store all my data when researching a keyword. This tool eliminated that and cut my search time down. I can look at the detail listings to check for false positives very quickly. I start with KDP Rocket, and then I use KDSpy to confirm that I'm on to something.

The more I use KDP Rocket, the less I rely on KDSpy lately. The more I play around with Rocket, the more it's becoming my favorite tool. I have some videos of me using book tools in action at ServeNo-Master.com/orbit if you want to see the difference.

5

KEYWORD RESEARCH

I f you don't want to use any tools, Amazon's search box is amazing. When you start typing something in that box, Amazon will start trying to guess what your final term will be. This autocomplete will give you loads of great ideas.

Let's say we're doing a book on yoga. You love yoga, and it's your passion. Go into the search box and type "yoga a." Amazon will then give you a load of results starting with yoga anatomy, yoga accessories, and yoga as medicine.

Once you write down these ten keywords, you type in "yoga b." You will get the more results. It's then time to analyze each keyword to see if it has books in the top 30,000. We always want keywords that generate sales. Amazon lets you attach seven keywords to your book listing, and you don't want to waste any of them.

KDP Rocket Shortcut

There are a few standalone Amazon keyword research tools out there, but most of them just automate this process. Those tools will give you ten results for each letter after your keyword. So you end up with two hundred and sixty keywords. That's pretty cool and gives you a decent baseline. You will find at least eighty percent of the valuable keywords that way.

But here's the problem. Autocomplete will not come up with any keywords that don't start with yoga. You will not find "hot yoga" or "learn yoga" with this technique. Amazon's suggestions never suggest words in front of what you typed, only after.

I just typed "yoga" into KDP Rocket, and it came up with core power yoga and bikram yoga. These are two powerful keywords that no other tool would have found. I love this tool!

Speed up with KDSpy

KDSpy speeds up the keyword analysis process. You can type in a complete keyword from your list and then click on your KDSpy icon. It will show you the book sales numbers in a few seconds. When you are grinding through hundreds of keywords, the time-savings becomes massive.

Each time you search a keyword in Amazon, KDSpy will give you color-coded advice in three categories: popularity, potential, and competition. Popularity tracks how many overall sales there are amongst these books. Potential looks at the amount of money you can make if you get a book onto this page. Competition looks at how tough the other books on the page are. If every book has over a thousand reviews and hundreds of pages, then you will see a red light.

The tool's advice is usually pretty solid. As a beginner, it's worth trusting those color-coded recommendations. When you see three greens, you have found a keyword you want to use.

Assessing the competition

There is nothing worse than entering a market where there is loads of money to be made and realizing that the competition it just too brutal. Books through massive publishing houses that have been bestsellers for decades are not easy to knock off their perches.

The second part of keyword research is checking out the competition. How many pages are the books? How many reviews do they have? What's the price point? How long has the book been around?

If I see twenty books that are all older than me, contain five hundred pages, and have thousands of reviews, I know that category is simply too tough for me. I don't want to spend tens of thousands of dollars on a marketing campaign to fight them. It's much better to find categories where the books have less than one hundred reviews, less than two hundred pages, and are less than five years old. Then I know it's a keyword or category with some movement or opportunity.

KDSpy can do the assessment for you with its green, yellow, red light system.

Keyword Limits

When you publish your book to Kindle, you are allowed to include seven relevant keywords. When you publish to Createspace, you only get five. Make a list of your best seven keywords, but also mark which are the two worst keywords; these are the ones that won't make it to the paperback listing.

CRAFTING A TITLE THAT SELLS

Writing a great book title is truly an art. Most books have terrible titles, and it kills their sales. I spent a long time brainstorming with a few of my interns to dial in the title of this book.

Start by looking at the books you will compete with. How are their titles structured? Do they have one-word titles, or are their titles just keywords? When you check on the "yoga" keyword, most of the top books are simply titled "Yoga." This is a space where titles are just keywords.

In fiction, this won't fly. Would anyone read a book called "Space Marines?" Would you buy a book called "Detective Story?"

Look at the way your competition structures their titles. For most non-fiction categories, the title is a keyword or a short phrase that leads into the keyword.

On a practical level, look at the top ten books in your area that are making decent money. Once you have the title structure dialed in, look for words that repeat. Look for terms that appear over and over again in their titles. That shows you the keywords they are targeting.

When working on the title for this book, I kept seeing timeframes in the titles. Write a book in three months, two months, thirty days, ten days, and even twenty-four hours. It appears that there is an arms race on writing the fastest books possible. When I checked on these keywords, however, I found that nobody types them into the Amazon search box. That's why my title doesn't have any time element.

Once you have dialed in the keywords that you want to appear in your title, start looking for images that fit the idea. I noticed that a lot of competing books have a picture of a pencil-rocket flying into outer space. This image is a little bit too cartoonish for me and doesn't quite sync up with my brand. I also don't want to copy what other people are doing.

I started looking at pictures of space and aliens and books and spaceships. I like the idea of launching a book. The word "launch" appears in titles over and over again. There is no synonym with the same power. "Release a book" just doesn't have the same energy.

I love reading science-fiction novels, as you well know, and in space navy books they always talk about the importance of controlling the high orbitals. In a gravity well, whoever holds the high ground is dominant. It's much easier to drop a rock from a spaceship than it is to shoot a rocket back up from the planet.

High orbital and gravity wells became the seed of my primary idea. After bouncing more ideas and looking at astronauts and spaceships, I came up with *Breaking Orbit*. I brainstormed this with some buddies and then I thought about "Break Orbit." Everyone preferred *Breaking Orbit* more, and that became the title of this book.

After the Colon

The subtitle is where you can go to town with your keywords. Find the highest performing keywords from your list and put them into a logical sentence. It's a balance between keyword stuffing and being ridiculous.

Some books go way too far and have a big list of keywords that looks ugly. The desire to rank for those terms has damaged the aesthetic of their Amazon listing and book cover. Finding the keywords is a science, but combining them in a way that sells books is an art.

My subtitle for this book doesn't have an exact match keyword. The top terms were "write a book," "publish a book," and "publish a bestseller." A robot would use the title *Write a Book: Publish a Book, Publish a Bestseller.* This title looks and reads horribly, but there are plenty of books on Amazon that look like this. Their titles scream "marketer" rather than value.

The second half of my subtitle came from reading reviews of the competition. I read some negative reviews that complained about getting a book out there without an existing following. My method assumes that you have no friends, family or following to boost your sales. I have entered multiple markets on Amazon with zero following.

Since my method answers this complaint, I decided to stick it into my title. With non-fiction, you want to make it as clear as possible what people will get when they read it. I like to provide clarity.

With fiction, you often have to explain the genre to potential readers. That's why many books say things like "a space cowboy shapeshifting thriller" in the subtitle. I know that seems silly to established authors, but that information affects a lot of buying decisions. Anytime I see "a supernatural detective" in the subtitle, I buy the book because I know what the book is about.

The Glory of the Word Cloud

KDSpy shines when creating book titles. When I have the top twenty books in my category on the page, I can click a word cloud button. The software analyzes all of the titles on the page and tells me the words that appear the most frequently among those titles.

I can shortcut my process with the click of a button.

TOOLS OF THE TRADE - OUTLINING

When I encounter a writer suffering from writer's block, I can always trace back their difficulties to the research phase. Whether you are writing fiction or non-fiction, lack of an outline can grind your entire project to a halt. I use two primary tools for my research and outlining phase.

You can use any method that works for your personality. When I began writing, I used a basic word processor for each stage of my process. Having written over one hundred books, my process is now more streamlined. I only add tools to my workflow if they save me money or increase my productivity.

Nothing else matters.

Xmind

I started mind-mapping a few years ago, and I've never looked back. Mind maps are outlines in a circular format. Everything expands out from the center, rather than in a straight line.

In school and working as a teacher, every system I used was linear. The order was locked in as you developed the content. I learned this system because it was the only one available to me. Transitioning to mind-mapping unlocked my creativity. It separates the content from the order and allows me to generate much better research.

I recommend trying mind-mapping and outlining to see which method suits your personality. Everyone is different and will prefer a different method.

I have been using Xmind for about two years now. It is absolutely free. There is a paid upgrade, but you don't need that. I used Xmind to outline the book you are reading right now. I do the majority of my outlining and planning in Xmind.

As I research, I save all my best ideas as little notes in the mind map. The order is very fluid. With a mind map, I can drag a branch around to change the order of the chapters. I don't come up with ideas and notes in the same order as the final book. As I write and go into later research, changing the order is really important to me. This fluidity is the reason I personally adore mind maps.

OmniOutliner

If you are a linear thinker, then you will prefer traditional outlining. My assistant loves to outline directly in Word. The thought of doing that makes me cringe, but it works for her. I haven't tried to force her to use either of these tools. Find what works for you and stick with it.

Sometimes I need to create a linear outline. I am working on several 30-day challenges. One of the projects is about setting up and making money from a blog in thirty days. There are thirty steps in that outline, so I used my outlining software, OmniOutliner Pro.

I only use this software for five percent of my outlining, so I can't give you a hard recommendation. I am blissfully ignorant of the competition, and I don't even know if there is a PC version. This is simply a tool that I bought ages ago and still use. It's easily the most expensive tool that I will mention in this entire book, so feel free to find a cheaper alternative.

I was just working on my 30-day challenge outline a few weeks ago in OmniOutliner. If you are a linear thinker, take a look around, and you can probably find an excellent free tool that meets your needs. When you do, please email me and I'll add it as a resource on my website.

BUILDING THE FRAMEWORK OF A BESTSELLER

Research and planning are the keys to any successful book. This section will share how I outline non-fiction books. Creating a fiction book is so complex that it requires a separate book. There are a few amazing books that I recommend for creating your fiction outline at ServeNoMaster.com/orbit.

Even if you are writing a fiction book, most of this section will still apply to you, as it is about creating the big picture or strategy for your book in a way that your audience will enjoy consuming.

Our audience will tell us what they want to read about. Then we simply give them what they want, using our own voice.

Mind Map or Outline

The research process starts with a mind map or an outline. You can choose either method, but you do need a place where you store data. In this process, we will save ideas, quotes, references to medical studies and other key pieces of information.

Our initial research process will help to generate a table of contents. Depending on your level of expertise with the subject, that might be all you need. When I'm writing on a new topic, I like to dig deep into my research. I look for original medical journals and studies. I want the first level information as much as possible.

For this book, my outline was mostly big picture. I research, write and publish new books every month, so I already knew the deeper content for each chapter. Whatever you are working on, the deeper you research, the better.

Reverse Engineer

The entire process of creating non-fiction books is to reverse engineer what the competition is doing. We want to read similar books, watch training videos, read scholarly research and forum posts. Take parts from dozens of resources to assemble the best content. Then streamline that material and add in your own voice.

Creating a book from research is much easier than starting from scratch. Trying to turn an idea into a book with no strategy or organization is tough. The deeper you delve into your research, the easier it will be when you start writing your book.

With a fiction book, you might only take a few big picture ideas from other books in your genre. With a non-fiction book, research is imperative. You want to delve into your research as deeply as possible.

Deconstructing the Table of Contents

Your mind map inner circle will become your table of contents. To develop this, begin by looking at the tables of contents in similar books that are doing well. Amazon allows you to look inside other books without even buying them. Every chapter topic you see in one of the top five relevant books gets added to your mind map. Start off going for quantity. You can easily pare down and merge chapter ideas later.

When you examine five different books, you will find that each book covers topics that the other ones don't. This is why you look at more than just one book. We want to create an amazing customer experience for our future readers. If a reader wants to learn the material that is in book A and book B, they have to buy both of them right now. When your book comes out, they can just buy yours and not need to look for additional information elsewhere.

Many people just copy the table of contents from one similar book and think this phase is done. Don't do that. You want to go deeper. This training is not about creating good books, it is about creating excellent ones.

Big Promises

Look at the sales pages of similar books and products. Read the descriptions of every book you are competing with that is doing well. What does it promise the reader? Fiction and non-fiction books alike make promises.

For many of the books I read, they promise a great space opera adventure, planet-hopping, space marine battles or great naval engagements in the depths of outer space. The descriptions of popular books will give you a feel of what your audience is looking for in a book.

The promises made on the sales page need to be answered by the content in your book. This applies across all genres and sales platforms. Violating a promise is the fastest way to lose your audience and get one-star reviews.

I used to read a great series about space marines. Each book followed a year in the life of the main soldier. For the first four books, the space marines fought aliens across glorious battlefields. In the fifth book, the series took a hard left turn. The marines were sent to guard factories owned by evil corporations and to kill human protestors.

The books had almost zero battles and turned into pure political commentary. The author set up a world where evil corporations owned entire planets and then spent the rest of the book trying to convince me that this is bad. I was on board with the idea from page one. I don't think corporations should own planets. The rest of the book was a complete waste. He promised me space marines and turned it into a political agenda.

He broke his promise, and if you find the author I'm talking about, you can see exactly where his series crashed. You can't break promises, and you can't change the story later in the series. The promises from book one have to remain through the entire series.

The majority of science-fiction is filled with political critique, and I enjoy all of it, but if I buy a book about space marines fighting aliens and instead get a book about space marines killing poor people and then feeling guilty about it, I'm going to be disappointed.

During my tinnitus research, I noticed that many of the books had a few initial good reviews, and then the following reviews savaged the authors. If you write a book about curing tinnitus, your cure better work.

Look at the promises made on other sales pages and add those to your outline. Make sure that you can meet each of those promises, and you will get loads of five-star reviews from happy readers.

One-Star Reviews

People either love or hate most books. The five-star reviews tell me everything I need to know about the book. They will point out the best aspects of the book and how the audience connected. Sometimes the top reviews will be about the main character, the personal stories or the scientific footnotes.

A five-star review is written by a reader who felt the book met all the promises on the sales page. The book kept its word, and now the reader is sharing that with the world. The five-star reviews reveal the content that your book absolutely must contain to compete.

The one-star reviews, however, reveal opportunity in the market. My goal with every book I write is to turn all the one-star reviews for other books into five-star reviews for mine. They tell me the sections that were missing from the other book; the promises unfulfilled and the questions unanswered. These dissatisfied customers are a gold mine.

If I can satisfy the competition's happy and unhappy reviewers, I have a book that can dominate the market.

A one-star review gave me the idea for my subtitle.

Less than ten percent of the reviews for a successful book will be one-stars. Don't think of this as appeasing the smallest segment; you are creating a superior product.

A wise author plays the same game with their own books. This book will get some bad reviews. No matter how good your book is, somebody will hate it. Instead of getting upset with the reviewer, a good author uses that review to improve the book. If a reviewer complains that the book doesn't cover something they expected, add that to your book.

The beauty of controlling your publishing is the speed with which you can change and update your content. I can update a book and push the content to all of my platforms within twenty-four hours. That's how quickly I can adapt to a bad review. You don't want to give your future competition any easy opportunities down the line.

Building a Skeleton

The research process can be incredibly detailed, and I go far deeper into my techniques on my website, but you have enough right now to put together a pretty great book. I think of my mind map as a monster. The inner layer begins with the keyword research and the promises my book will answer. This is the brain of my monster.

My second round of research creates the table of contents. I create the skeleton of my monster and organize the structure of my content. Sometimes a few bones get out of place, and the mind map makes it very easy to put them where they belong.

Once the skeleton is in place, I get into my "deep research phase."

Instead of reading sales pages and the table of contents, go deep. Read the top books on Amazon. Go through the best courses on Clickbank and Udemy. Whatever you do, do NOT copy and paste someone else's words into your book. You never want to plagiarize. But you do want to see what's out there.

If you research this deeply, you will be a pretty good author. But we want more than pretty good; we want to achieve greatness. To go deeper, read the top forums on your topic. Find the questions that people ask the most often, and add that content to your book.

With every book, product, and article you examine, ALWAYS find the original research. I use Google Scholar every single day. Modern blog posts often footnote poorly. Sometimes they mention the school and year where the study was performed. It takes a little digging, but I want that source material.

Take the time to read the introduction and the conclusion of the original researchers. Many of their conclusions get twisted as bloggers and reporters copy each other. Some research is run through a game of Telephone before you find it. Telephone was the game I played as a child where each one would whisper a message to the child next to them. By the time the message passed around the circle, it was nothing like the original.

Once you've found that core research, take a look at later articles and research on the subject or by the same authors. If you can see through the fog, you can create some brilliant content.

Here is an example of Telephone. During World War II, the Pope actively fought to save as many people from the German tyranny as possible. He was considered a near-saint at the time, and after World War II the Russians hated him for that. They launched a disinformation campaign to convince the world that the Pope was pro-Nazi.

You will not find a single article written before 1950 that speaks ill of the Pope. Every single piece sings his praises for fighting so hard to save so many people.

But now you see stories, even in fiction books, that call that Pope a Nazi. These authors fell for a piece of Russian propaganda and made the story worse and worse with each retelling. Anything other than the original study or source material is always suspect. As with everything else, you can find the source material for this Pope story at ServeNoMaster.com/orbit.

Putting it all Together

Once you have your deep outline and references assembled, you are ready to move forward with your book creation process. The more material on your mind map or outline, the easier the actual writing process becomes. If you run into writer's block, the most likely culprit is incomplete research.

Some people are tempted to research and write at the same time. Going back and forth between learning and creating will slow down your process. Your brain has to switch between creating and receiving information constantly. These switches will cost you lots of time.

That is why the research sections of this book are so long and come first. An hour spent researching will often save you ten when writing.

9

BECOMING AN AUTHOR

Choosing the right name for your author is crucial. Do you want your name permanently attached to this topic? Will your audience respond to your name? Most movie stars change their names. They know that the right name can magnify a career.

You might want to write a series of children's books and a series of books about physics. You want to isolate those two series from each other using pen names. I'm using my real name on this book, but I have used many pen names in the past.

When someone clicks on your name on Amazon, they get taken to your author page. If they see a bunch of books that don't make sense together, you might turn them off. Imagine clicking on the author profile of your favorite romance author and seeing a bunch of children's books. You aren't going to buy any of them, and you are going to be confused.

In general, I prefer to use a pen name. It puts some space between you and your author identity. It provides a layer of security and privacy as you get bigger. It allows you to create a persona that matches your audience.

Choosing a Pen Name

To choose a pen name I head over to the census website. The federal government keeps a list of the most popular names from each year and each decade. During my research in a market, I get a feel for the age of my author. Some of my authors were born in the seventies, and some were born in the fifties. I choose an age that will increase sales of my book and improve the connection to my audience.

You want a pen name with two first names, like Michael David. Everyone in your target age bracket will know a Michael or a David. That feeling that they know someone with the same name will give a little boost to your sales numbers.

Go through the list and combine popular names of the correct age. Then check to see if the website for that name is available. You want to own your author's name as much as possible. If I can't get MichaelDavid.com, I move on.

Owning the domain name for your author will make life a lot easier as you grow. I started this book telling you that we are building a business. This step is the foundation for that business. When you have twenty books and are trying to sell coaching, you will be very disappointed when the only website left is The-Michael-David.net. You know that nobody will ever spell that right, and you will lose a lot of customers.

The Importance of Gender

How many people would buy a romance novel or a book on breast-feeding from a male author? Would you buy a book on male puberty written by a woman?

As much as we don't want to admit it, the gender of the author affects sales in nearly every market. The only way to overcome having the wrong gender for a market is to put Dr. in front of your name.

Do not do this when creating a pen name. If you aren't a doctor, then your pen name isn't either.

Choose the gender that sells best in your market and you will see a bump in sales.

Choosing Your Author Image

To get an image for your newly invented author, you can go to a stock image site and buy something for a buck. A large proportion of the author images you see on Amazon were purchased this way. Many of the books on Amazon are now by pen names, and many authors prefer to maintain a layer of anonymity.

Your other option is a drawing. There is a trend among romance authors to simply have a drawing for their profile picture. They don't even bother using a photograph.

You only need one picture to use across all your social media locations, so choose one that you like. And in case you decide to check right now, yes, the picture on my Author Central profile is me. This book is not written under a pseudonym.

Foundations of Greatness

Part of becoming a successful author is planning for the future. This book is about much more than launching a single book; this is about building an entire empire around your book. You are going to create a real business here, and planning for the future is crucial.

Sometimes people go on television to talk about their new product. They get way more attention than they expected and their website crashes, or they run out of stock. They lose tens or even hundreds of thousands of dollars because they didn't expect or prepare for success.

That is not how I operate or how I teach.

Before you launch your first book, you want to put your secondary properties in place. Set up your website and social media accounts. This is a demonstration that you believe you will succeed. You don't have to build out the properties just yet, but controlling the names will be important.

Imagine if you have a successful book and somebody out there grabs all the social media names and the website. That would dramatically hurt your business. You don't want to leave yourself vulnerable to something like that.

After you launch your first book, you will have time to build out your pages more. For now, we just want to stake our claim.

10

TOOLS OF THE TRADE - WRITING

I don't know if I'm the fastest writer in the entire world. There's always somebody better. But I do very well. I started writing this book today, and I've already pumped out nearly twelve thousand words. Many days I generate twenty thousand words.

A big part of writing fast is having the correct foundation.

You now know my research process. With a deep outline, writing the actual content is a breeze. You just fill in the space between each point. The creativity is no longer stressful. You know where you are and where you are going.

With a great outline, you need a great tool to take advantage of it. There is no word processor better than Scrivener. I write everything in Scrivener, from books to blog posts to book descriptions. I'm writing this book inside of Scrivener right now. I sing the praises of this product on my podcast, on my blog, and in my other books.

It's the centerpiece of my business, and I have put more than one million words through it. That's the ultimate testimonial. Scrivener speeds up your process and allows you to create an outline inside your document. Focusing on one tiny section at a time keeps you from feeling overwhelmed. The thought of writing an entire book and looking at a blank page is terrifying. Scrivener replaces that fear with confidence.

As you finish each section, you get a feeling of accomplishment. You turn the mammoth task of writing an entire book into manageable chunks. You can focus on writing one chapter at a time without getting distracted by the overall size of your project.

My entire business is built on this software.

It does have one weakness: the spell-check is garbage. Don't rely on it.

During the writing phase, don't worry about spelling. We'll cover how to deal with spelling, grammar, and editing after you have finished your book.

11

WRITE LIKE THE WIND

W e are not creating something from nothing. That approach to writing is very hard and stressful. By outlining in advance, you are in a position for fast and efficient writing. Writing a book following this method is similar to playing the game "connect the dots." You have all the waypoints in your book mapped out already. As you write each section, you only focus on getting from point A to point B. Turning the overwhelming project of writing a book into a series of small tasks makes it manageable and achievable.

We have the skeleton of our outline and the muscles from our in-depth research. Now it's time to sew the skin on this monster and bring it to life. Focus on one small section at a time and you will never get overwhelmed. Right now I'm only writing this part and not thinking about the next one. I'll deal with that only when this one is finished.

Write your book one step at a time.

How Long Should My Book Be?

During the research phase, we looked at a lot of data. One key piece of information we gathered was the length of our competition. If all of your competitors write two-hundred-page books, then that's the window you should target.

When I sat down to write this book, I set a goal of 25,000 words. That was my initial goal based on researching the competition, but from the way this is going, I think this book will be a lot longer. There's just nothing I can cut out. I don't want to hold anything back.

Do the best to meet the expectations of your audience. It is better to go too long than to go too short. If needed you can trim down the book-length during the editing process. Once you have your initial target word count, you can create a writing calendar.

Create a Writing Calendar

The average bestseller on Amazon is around ten thousand words long. For this section, let's imagine that your book will be ten thousand words long. Take the days between now and your target completion date and divide by your desired book length.

If you wanted to write a ten-thousand-word book in thirty days, this comes out to just three hundred and thirty-three words a day. That assumes you write seven days a week. That is a little overwhelming for some people. If you just work weekdays, you can write your first draft in four weeks. That's pretty great!

Part of creating a writing calendar is the hours you have available. If you can only write for thirty minutes per day, five hundred words might not be achievable yet. I have a longer and more detailed book about writing fast called "20K a Day." It's coming out after this one, and I've already completed the deep outline. Together we are going to continue to refine and improve your writing process.

If you push yourself too hard, you can burn out and overwhelm yourself. Writing fast is a skill, and it takes time and practice to develop. I find that a target of five hundred words a day is achievable for first-time writers. Give yourself a two-hour block every day, or every weekday, and use that time to hit your daily goal.

Writing with a plan allows you to set up your book for prerelease properly, and you can give real dates to people.

If someone asks when your book is coming out, they will appreciate a real date a lot more than a vague answer.

Talk to Text

Not everyone is a maestro with the keyboard.

Most of us talk much faster than we type. There are many ways to create books using dictation. I have written several long blog posts breaking down the process and the technological options if you want to go down this path, but allow me to give you the highlights here.

The average person speaks between one hundred and one hundred fifty words per minute. If you record yourself speaking each section and chapter of your book, you can generate six thousand words per hour. You could speak your entire book in less than two hours. This is the secret technique behind those "write a book in a day" promises. I didn't even make that promise on my sales page, and I'm still keeping it!

Tons of smartphone apps will record your voice and generate rough transcription for you. They aren't perfect, but they are getting closer all the time. Macintosh comes with a built in transcriber, and there is some more expensive software out there as well.

Most transcription software stinks at punctuation, so you will have to spend more time editing your book. The time trade-off is pretty good, though.

Another option is to record your entire book into a voice recorder and send it to a service. The service I use costs $1 a minute and will transcribe with proper punctuation. They are about 99% accurate, so very minimal editing is required. This is a great solution if that is in your budget.

I thought about dictating this entire book, but my house is way too loud right now. Plus, I record five podcast episodes a week. My voice needs a little break.

If writing seems daunting to you, then I wholeheartedly recommend dictating your book. I work with many people who use this process, and they create amazing books fast.

Writing Location

Whether writing or speaking your book, location is critical. Your time is very precious, and I don't want to waste any of it. You need a space where you will not be disturbed for your entire writing time block.

I live with two kids, a dog and lots of insanity. My newborn son has very little regard for my work, and cries whenever he is hungry. I can't tell him to be quiet. He's a baby.

When I'm deep into writing, I wear my green headphones. My family knows that I wear these headphones when I'm working on something important, and they don't disturb me.

Some people like to write at a coffee shop. I just can't write in public like that. I get very distracted, and my writing slows down. Right now I'm at my desk, facing the ocean through a giant window. I get to see paradise, but distractions are kept to a minimum.

Your writing location should be sacrosanct. Write in the same location every time and you will begin to train your mind. When you sit down at your writing location and put on your writing headphones, your brain knows that it's time to get serious and focus.

Writing Time of the Day

Some people write in the morning, and some write in the evening. Everyone is different. Your time may be controlled by your work schedule or your personality. I prefer to write earlier in the day because I write faster in the morning than I do in the evening.

My writing sessions start early in the morning. I know my rhythm, and I work with my body. Trying to fight yourself is just too hard.

It might take a little while to find the rhythm that works best for you. If this is your first writing project, experiment a little to find the best time for you to write. Once you find your optimal writing time, stick to writing at the same time every day. Writing at the same time of day will ensure that your book maintains consistent quality.

Burnout

Every writer is different. Some people can only write five hundred words a day, while others can write twenty thousand without breaking a sweat. Trying to push yourself for higher word counts too fast can become counterproductive.

When you are working there will come a moment when you notice your attention fading. The quality of your sentences drops. Your body is showing the first warning signs that you are out of gas.

It's tempting to push yourself, to keep grinding until you hit your target word count, but this is a mistake. You will exhaust your brain, risking burnout. The quality of your work will diminish. You might crank out a few more pages or chapters, but during the editing process you will have to rewrite most of this content. You are saving time now that will cost you far more time in the future.

In 20K a Day, I cover extensive speed-writing techniques and how to increase your daily word counts. Writing is a skill, and you train to develop it, just like going to the gym. If you start by adding to your target each day, you will strengthen your writing muscles. If you start out writing five hundred words on Monday, shoot for five hundred and ten on Tuesday. Stay there for a few days and try five-twenty on Friday.

Each time you increase your word count, stay at that level for a few days before you push yourself again. It might not seem like big changes, but after a month you could be at six hundred words a day. That is a twenty percent increase in your productivity. That is a massive gain!

Routine and Ritual

I'm a big believer in the power of ritual. I like to create rituals to bring my body and mind into alignment before I write. A ritual is simply the act you perform before each writing session.

Your pattern might start when you come home from work. You know you are going to write, so you begin to prepare yourself. You eat dinner and then start your ritual. First, you take a shower to remove the smell of the office from your body and to cleanse your mind. Then you put on your favorite writing sweatpants and make a cup of tea. You toast a bagel and take your writing snack to your special nook.

You put on your special blue headphones and sit down at your desk. You fire up the computer and read your favorite comic for ten minutes. Once you are caught up and you have a little entertainment inside you, you open Scrivener and begin writing. Writing comes naturally; every step in your ritual moved you closer to your writing state, that mental place where the words just flow from your body.

My personal ritual is different because I write in the mornings. I follow the same steps every single day before I begin writing. After checking my email, reading my favorite two comics, and catching up on the news, I fire up Scrivener. My pre-writing tasks take thirty minutes or less, and that gives my brain time to wake up and shake off the cobwebs.

Once I start writing it is very easy for me to stay in the zone. My body knows this pattern. Just like athletes warm up before they step into the arena, I warm up before I start writing. Ritual is very powerful. Choosing a consistent time and location to write is the foundation of your writing ritual. Develop a pattern that works for you and lock into it.

My ritual is why I don't experiment with new pieces of software very often. I am aware that there are other writing tools out there that compete with Scrivener in different ways. Plenty of people love those tools and swear by them. I am locked into my personal ritual, and I only make changes when there will be a large spike in productivity.

Time is a precious commodity, and anything that gives me back more time is valuable.

Writer's Block

I've never experienced writer's block. I know that makes me sound like a pretentious know-it-all, but please give me a moment to elucidate.

Large-scale writer's block is when you are staring at a page and have no idea what to write about next. You are sitting in front of a typewriter with a blank page loaded up and have no idea what key to press first.

The smaller version of writer's block is when you know what you want to say, but you can't find the words. You can envision how you want the scene or chapter to play out, but you're stuck on how to make it happen. You want to get your hero from the garden to the castle, but you just can't feel the right path yet.

The cure to big picture writer's block is outlining and research. If you have your plan in place before you start writing, the steps are easy.

You can see exactly where this section is going. In my tiny window right now, I am writing my section about writer's block. I'm done thinking about ritual, and I won't think about outsourcing until I open those windows. I had to look at my folders to even see the previous and next section topics. My mind locks into a tiny task and stays there until it is completed.

When you have a deeply researched and well-structured outline, you always know what to write about next.

Sometimes a single scene or chapter has you trapped with micro-writer's block. You know where you want to go but just can't seem to write the words to get you there. When you're stuck here, Scrivener is awesome. You just skip the scene.

This book is organized into approximately twenty folders which will eventually be my chapters. Each folder has five to ten little files that will become headings within the chapter. If I'm stuck, I just go work on something different. It doesn't happen very often, but when it does I leave that part for a later date. Sometimes I need to do more research, and sometimes I just need to let my brain rest.

When I come back the next day, I'm able to tackle that chapter without problems.

The order of chapters can be very fluid as you create your story. I've already written half of a section in the final chapter of this book. I was writing about Clickbank, and I started to go off topic. It happens. I just moved the file to a later part of the book.

Nobody cares how fast you wrote your book. They don't care about the order in which you wrote it. Your audience can't tell. They think of a book in terms of how long it took them to read it. For some people, this is a one-day book. Some people read very fast. For others, this book may take several weeks, and they think of this book as much longer. For them, it is a project and a commitment.

Your readers only care about the finished product and their experience. Give them a great experience and write the chapters in any order you feel like!

Outsourcing

Perhaps you grabbed this book because you want to build a writing empire. You want to sell books, not write them. That's understandable. Using ghostwriters can speed up your entire process. You can generate multiple books simultaneously and grow your business much faster.

There are several challenges with hiring ghostwriters, mostly built around price, speed, and quality. You can hire a phenomenal writer, but if they take two years to write one book, that won't help your business very much.

Some people jump into the Kindle game and pay someone in another country to write their book for under a hundred bucks.

They start cranking out books as fast as they can and are shocked when the negative reviews start rolling in. Is a thirty-three-page book really a book?

Sometimes a very short book is valuable. When you take a big subject and break it down for your customers, shorter can be better. But I don't believe in corner-cutting when it comes to content.

A few bad reviews can kill a book, a pen name, and eventually your entire Amazon account. When you hire the cheapest writers you can find, you will have books filled with spelling and grammatical mistakes. On the PSAT, I scored a perfect in the English section. I didn't make a single mistake, and yet my books are littered with typos before I edit. There is an excellent chance that someone will find an error that slipped through the cracks and email me about it. When that happens, I fix the mistake and upload the new version to Amazon.

When you hire a discount writer, you have to do a LOT of editing to bridge the gap. My last book, Serve No Master, is just over ninety thousand words. I wrote the first draft of the book in four days, but I spent more than one hundred hours on editing and rewrites. Editing is a much slower process than writing. Writing is about letting the words flow and unlocking your creativity. Editing is about being laser-focused and fastidious. (I'll teach you how to edit faster in the next chapter.)

You can hire good talent when you have a definite plan in place. I have a template you can use to hire writers; just reply to one of my emails and ask for it. In general, a decent writer will charge 2-8 cents per word. There is a range and depends on the project scope. You can hire a decent non-fiction writer for a ten books that are ten thousand words each. This writer will cost you around two grand.

When you hire writers for one book at a time, the price will go up. That's just the nature of the beast.

The primary place to hire writers right now is UpWork. Most of the freelance writing websites merged into a single source.

Even when hiring another writer, I prefer to handle the initial outline myself.

You don't want to publish a book that you haven't read or don't understand. Releasing content without being on top of your game is risky. One of my friends purchased some cheap content, threw it on

Amazon, got flagged for plagiarism, and now he's banned for life. He didn't steal the words, one of his employees did. When you are the boss, the buck always stops at your doorstep. You can't blame the outsourcer when you get caught with stolen content.

You can certainly hire other people to write your books, and I'll continue adding more content to my website covering this topic in greater detail. Whether you write the book yourself or hire someone else, you want to handle the editing phase correctly.

12

TOOLS OF THE TRADE - EDITING

G rammarly is the most glorious tool in my entire collection. It might not be able to replace a human editor, but this tool will correct at least eighty percent of the mistakes a human editor would catch. I wrote one of the longest blog posts of my life reviewing this tool and breaking down the hundreds of reasons that I love it.

Grammarly connects to a central server and scans your writing for loads of errors, mistakes and just plain wordiness. I straight up love this tool, and EVERYTHING I write gets run through this before anyone else sees it. It scans my blog posts for me in real time and ensures that I don't look like a dumb-dumb because of some typos. No matter how much we want to deny it, typos make us think the writer is dumb.

Grammarly works perfectly with Scrivener. I pull one section at a time to edit. I can keep my editing process laser-focused and avoid feeling overwhelmed by the thought of hours and hours of editing. Editing in this way creates loads of stopping points. It's very easy to stop between sections when you get tired.

I cannot speak the praises of Grammarly enough. The tool is always improving and growing. Each time I use it, I can see that the software is getting smarter. Eventually, Grammarly may achieve sentience and start sending robots back in time to kill our heroes, but until that day comes this tool is pure gold for the independent writer.

Hemingway

If you write fiction, Hemingway is not optional. You must grab this tool. We have a tendency to write wordy sections that just take far too long to get to the point. Unfortunately, most of your audience reads at a third-grade level. If your writing is too long and complicated, your audience will get turned off. They might even think you are pretentious.

Hemingway looks at your sentences and tells you to cut it out. This wonderful little tool analyzes each sentence and assigns a color. You know exactly where to chop things down. Personally, I use Grammarly a lot more than Hemingway, but at ten bucks right now this guy is a total steal.

I am testing Hemingway on more of my projects, and for fiction it is simply crucial.

Word

Though it might surprise you, my books do eventually end up in Word. I hate writing in Word, but this is where I do a lot of my final blocking and formatting. My books go through Word before they end up in CreateSpace.

Once my book has been through my entire editing process, Word is the final step. I run the built-in Spelling and Grammar check across the entire document. Word will catch mistakes that Grammarly misses, as the algorithm works in a different way. Eventually, Grammarly will become so smart that I don't need Word, but right now a final scan is worth it.

Word sends in some false positives, but it's worth the effort. The more mistakes you can catch via automation, the better.

13

EDITING

The Kiss of Death

There is one type of review that can murder a book. When someone leaves a review pointing out the bad grammar and spelling in a book, that book will die. It's the sniper bullet that kills new books from a thousand yards. Some reviewers think they are being helpful by pointing out that the author couldn't afford an editor but really should have used one anyway.

This review is honest, but it's also brutal. You must do everything in your power to avoid one of these. Cutting corners in your book creation or outsourcing process will leave you with a book riddled with errors. This book right now is loaded with errors. I'm in the initial writing phase. But there is no way on earth I would release it onto Amazon in this state.

Spend as much on editing as you can afford. Some editors are brutally expensive, and you have no choice but to do it yourself. Do your best and get friends and family to help you as well. Do whatever it takes to avoid getting the "death review."

I read a new book every day. I am a voracious reader, but when I see one of these reviews I still won't read the book. Even as someone who knows how hard handling the editing process on your own can be, I still move on. Do not screw around with the editing process or you might end up with the mark of death on your Amazon listing.

Edit Yourself

I handle the first round of editing my books myself. Whether you are going to hire an editor or handle everything yourself, your book should go through this phase.

If you hire a writer, you still need to edit the book. No writer will deliver a perfectly edited book. There is a reason that editors exist.

If you look around online, many editors hate on Grammarly. They write about how the tool can't replace a real, human editor. That's entirely accurate. A human editor will do a better job, but not everyone can afford that.

Wait at least a week between finishing your book and beginning the editing process. The second you write the final word in the final chapter, you may be tempted to roll back to the start of your book and immediately begin editing. Don't do that; your brain is still in writing mode.

Waiting a week before you start any editing allows your brain time to relax, and you will start to forget your book. When you start editing, you will be able to look at each chapter with fresh eyes rather than only remembering when you wrote it a few hours earlier. Memory can become a major distraction when you edit too soon.

I start my personal process with Grammarly and run the entire book through that software before I do anything else. Grammarly helps me with the spelling and grammar, but it also helps me with my language. Like Hemingway, it points out overly wordy sentences and chastises me every single time I dare to use passive voice. For Grammarly, passive voice is the greatest of sins.

With a work of fiction, you then need to run your book through Hemingway. Even for non-fiction, it's worth it. The tool will help to bring your sentences alive.

Many ghostwriters can put together decent content, but their final phrasing is imperfect. They send you a book that is good, but not great. Running the book through Hemingway will help you turn their words into pure gold.

Get as many people to read your book as possible if you are editing yourself. Give away loads of free copies and ask people to email you if they catch a mistake that slipped through the cracks. You can do your best and then use your profits from the first book sales to hire an editor for the second edition.

Hiring an Editor

Finding a good editor is tough. You can run Internet searches and read through author forums; you still might have no idea on pricing and competency.

When you contact an editor, they send you a complicated structure asking if you want editing, line-editing, or developmental editing. Their entire pricing structure is based on how much they will change your book.

Line editing focuses on communication and will point out mistakes in language, redundancies, and other bigger picture mistakes. Copy editing is focused purely on spelling and grammar errors. This process is far more technical. There are also proofreaders and many other types of editors to deal with.

It's a daunting process and can end up costing thousands of dollars. How do you know which type of editing you need unless they have looked at your book? Most freelance editors start out at $.002 a word and go up from there in pricing. Line editing starts out close to $.01. For a book that is one hundred thousand words, line editing will cost at least a thousand bucks. That's a lot of cheddar for a book that's going to sell for $2.99.

When you make two bucks a sale, the first five hundred sales belong to your editor. It's a real kick in the teeth. Bad reviews if you don't do it, and no profits if you do. Trying to follow the traditional "publisher" advice leaves you paying out of pocket for multiple editors and proofreaders. You can easily spend ten thousand dollars before anyone sees your book.

Edit the book to the best of your ability using friends, family, and software. After that, there are some reasonably priced editors out there. If you have a short, ten-thousand-word book, you can find a decent editor for under two hundred bucks who can handle the job in a week.

Whatever you do, expect this process to take a bit of time. Writing is about creativity, but editing is about perfection. There are a few reasonably priced editors that I know, and I will post links to them at ServeNoMaster.com/orbit.

14

JUDGE A BOOK BY ITS COVER

Before readers ever see your book description, the inside pages or any reviews, they see your book cover on Amazon. A bad grammar review from a reader can kill your book, but a bad cover can ensure that you never sell a single copy.

I can look at a cover and immediately tell who made the cover. Bad covers are obvious and have glaring, unprofessional mistakes.

You must understand how customers purchase books on Amazon before you release your book. Many authors throw a book on Amazon, but they have never purchased one before. I meet a lot of struggling writers who don't own a Kindle.

Failure to understand your audience and how they make buying decisions will destroy your sales process. You can write the greatest book in the world, but if the cover is bad nobody will ever read it. More than ninety percent of buying decisions are controlled by the book cover.

I am doing my best to explain just how important this is here because I know exactly what will happen if you ignore me. I was on a coaching call today with a writer complaining about his book's lack of sales. The book cover was horrendous. The book had a mix of clashing neon colors that almost made my eyes tear up. The author's name was not on the cover. There was a pile of clipart that had nothing to do with the topic smashed on top.

If you ignore this chapter, your book will not sell. Do not email me complaining that my process doesn't work if you skip this step. You have to follow each step in this process to achieve success. Anything less and you will be disappointed.

I will say this one final time.

Nobody buys books with bad covers.

Purpose

Your cover can only serve one purpose. You cannot make a cover with two goals in mind, or your will fail at both of them. If you ask one hundred random independent authors about the purpose of their cover, most of them would give answers like,
- To be pretty
- To be interesting
- To show readers the story
- To show my name
- To draw attention
- To be exciting

All of those answers are fine... unless you want to sell books and make money. The cover of your book serves a purpose: to get potential readers to click on your Amazon listing.

You can't make your cover decision in isolation. Pretending that other books don't exist ensures that your book won't see the light of day. When your book appears on Amazon, it will be surrounded by other similar books. Potential customers will scroll past ten or twenty relevant books. We want your cover to be the one each potential reader decides to click on.

Even if your book is number one in your category, they will still see ten or twenty other books on the page that are all competing for that same customer. If they don't click on your book and go to your listing, there is a zero percent chance they will read your book.

They can only click on one book at a time, and you want to make sure your book gets that initial click. Your description and the elements of your actual listing page will turn that click into a sale.

Your cover will never sell the book by itself. People see attractive covers all the time for books that they don't buy.

If your book cover is too different from the competition, people will ignore it. If this were a romance novel, I would have a picture of a muscleman showing off his abs. That would make sense in that category, but there is no chance you would have bought this book if the cover was a nice set of abs. The abs would be fascinating and certainly have caught your attention. If my only goal was to get your attention, then I accomplished my mission.

But that's not my goal, and that's not your goal. Your cover is there to compete with other books and get you that click.

We want to be laser-focused and keep our exact goal in mind as we make each decision in assembling the marketing for the book.

Color

Choosing the colors for your book is an art form. I have colors that I enjoy the most, but they never make it onto my covers. My book is not an altar to my hubris. The book is designed to entice, entertain and inform the reader. The cover of this very book was designed to please you, not me.

There are a couple of critical decisions when choosing your color scheme. Start by looking at other books in your category or niche. Are all of the covers brightly colored, or do they use pastels? Do you see neon colors? Is the main background color black or white? For some spaces, all of the books use yellow as the dominant color.

You can go deep into color research. There are massive corporations that create and test color schemes to sell to other companies. Lots of research goes into the color of every single logo you see driving down the street. Colors and schemes are never chosen at random.

This book is in black and white, so including a bunch of demo color swatches here wouldn't be very informative. I have an entire lesson on my site showing how color works and why some colors clash and some drive the sale. Each color has an attached emotional feeling, and you don't want a color scheme that conflicts with the message of your book.

When choosing a design, I usually start with a single color that I want and allow my designer to create the rest of the design with complementary colors. It's easier to let a professional handle the color combinations. Limit your cover to four colors total, including black and white. Too many colors transitions from informative to appearing busy or distracting.

Black and White

More than half of all book purchases made on Amazon are through a Kindle device.

When you don't own a Kindle, you have no idea what the customer experience is and can make some big mistakes. Most people will see your cover initially at around one and a half by two inches in size. Your book cover will be slightly larger than a postage stamp.

On the Amazon website, the book will appear slightly larger, but not by much.

We get excited about our ideas and put together covers that look awesome full-size. That's great! But many covers that look awesome when big look like garbage when small.

When people encounter your book on Kindle, the image will be tiny, and it will be in black and white. Ninety-nine percent of authors never test what their cover looks like in black and white. If you have a cover that is all beautiful blues and greens, on a Kindle it will appear muddy. Your cover will look like a black square, and nobody will take you seriously.

You absolutely must test your cover ideas in black and white before building your final cover concept. The key is to have colors with high contrast; you want colors that are very bright and very dark.

If you go back and look at my cover on your Kindle, you'll notice that it looks BETTER in black and white.

During the design phase, I made several changes that decreased how nice the cover looks large and in color. This cover is designed to look better small and in monochrome. The white smoke below the rocket ship pops right out of the page in black and white. Orange becomes the secondary color and white controls the screen.

With an orange title and a white sub-headline, people might not even be able to read my title on a small Kindle screen.

During the design phase of this book, I sent my concept out to three different artists. Each of them sent me a different design. I tested them all in black and white to choose my favorite.

If your cover doesn't work in black and white, you can slash your potential sales in half. If you already have a book that's struggling on Amazon, you should check your cover right now; it's the first thing I check with my coaching students.

Congruency

Earlier I mentioned the idea of putting a very muscular man with fantastic abs on the cover. The cover would be interesting, but nobody would click on the book, let alone buy it. The problem is one of congruency.

The art and images on your book must match the title and genre of your book. If you look at most books on Amazon after searching for "write a book," you'll notice there is no consistency. There are images of a giant eye, people sitting at typewriters, hot air balloons, a lot of pencils, and loads of books with the pages flapping in the wind. Most of these images have something to do with writing. The images make sense in the context of the topic.

The hot air balloon is floating out of a picture of a book, and the title is about writing children's books. In the correct context, even the hot air balloon makes sense.

If you scroll through your search results, you'll find some books that have a picture of the author on the cover. This is interesting because it's different, but none of these books have high sales numbers. The image has nothing to do with the topic.

There are certain books where we expect to see the author on the cover, such as diet and fitness books. Just because an idea works in one category does not mean it will work in another.

Authors are not traditional celebrities. I bet you can describe the features of less than ten successful authors. I don't think I can do more than ten. Authors are famous for their words, not their features.

A break in congruency can lose you the sale. Any time the picture on your book doesn't make sense to a reader, they might move on. People don't like to be confused.

You can ask for some feedback on your cover, and when somebody says they can't quite put their finger on it but something doesn't work for them, you have a congruency issue.

I went through a load of image ideas while I was creating the title for this book. During my brainstorming session, I bandied around potential titles and images with one of my interns. After testing out a few concepts, one of the images that I initially liked was an astronaut in outer space. The image had a high contrast ratio, and I knew it would pop in color and in black and white.

When he told me that he wasn't feeling that astronaut image but wasn't sure why, I knew it was a congruency issue. The main phrase we use is "launch a book." That is the seed phrase for the concept of writing and publishing a successful book. The word "launch" conveys the idea of a moment and the idea of success. We launch winners.

I took the idea of a spaceship from the word launch. We launch spaceships all the time. From there the idea grew into different space images. I looked at astronauts on foreign planets, but I knew immediately it was too far. I want to be related to the word "launch," but an astronaut on another planet is just way too strange.

I don't want to spend too much time talking about my covers; you can see the images that I considered for this book cover and why each of them failed at ServeNoMaster.com/orbit.

For your cover, find an image that is interesting enough to catch someone's eye, but not so far beyond the norm that it seems strange.

Designing covers is an art and should never be done in isolation. Get some feedback from the people around you or just post some choices to social media and let people comment. I often choose an image that is the wrong color and then hire an artist to create a version that has my desired color scheme.

This phase is purely about the shape and congruency of the image; I can easily change the colors later.

Planning for the Future

Most successful series have covers that look similar. With fitness books, authors usually have a single design, and each book is a different color. There will be a picture of the author in her workout clothes that matches the color scheme of the cover.

For one book she is in blue and the next she's in purple and then she wears green for book three. The more consistency you have between your book designs, the stronger your brand will become. When people see covers that look similar all the time, they start to give you more and more respect. They see your design enough times, and they will think that you're a celebrity author.

Your initial cover should be one that you can repeat as you release more books. Some books are very similar in title, and some are a little bit different. If you look at my fist book, Serve No Master, the book cover is slightly different. It's not a hard match, but there are a lot of consistencies. Both show an image of flight, have a simple image in between the title and author name, and have similar color schemes.

The books are related, but not part of a series.

I'm working on another book about writing fast. Because that book is so similar to this one, that cover will be much closer in design. I might simply take this cover and change around some of the colors to create consistency.

You don't have to design ten book covers before you launch the first one, but you do want to keep your future plans in mind. People like covers that are similar and make sense as part of a series. That feeling of familiarity builds trust and will increase your sales. You will also get a lot more customers who read the next book from your series as soon as they finish the first one.

Design Yourself

I am pretty decent at Photoshop. I know my way around layers and working with fonts, but no way would I ever try to design my cover. Unless you are an advanced graphic designer, I would recommend hiring a professional. I pay from five to twenty dollars for each of my covers.

I can get someone who designs book covers for a living very cheaply. It doesn't make sense for me to try and create my cover. I will create mock-ups and test different color schemes on my own during the cover creation process, but I always let a professional create the final project. Even if you are a phenomenal graphic artist, there are dozens of common pitfalls.

The font of your cover is critical. The right font can send your book into the stratosphere, but the wrong font can hurt your sales. It's not about aesthetics; there are plenty of beautiful fonts that can't sell a single book.

Proper placement and structure of the elements in your cover is vital. If the image looks off-center or is placed strangely between the title and subtitle, it might look cool to an artist. But it will cause one of those moments where people aren't sure why, but the covers feels weird to them. You can break congruency. People expect the elements of cover to be organized in a certain way.

If you are an artist creating a children's book, you may want to use one of your images on the cover. That's wonderful. You are very talented, and I work with several brilliant artists who write children's books. There is a huge difference between creating beautiful characters and mastering typography. Some artists purely specialize in text-based images and design.

Take your design and hire a cover designer to convert it into a compelling cover that sells loads of your beautiful book.

However, if you decide to create your own cover, upload it to my

Facebook page, and I'll personally leave a comment below it filled with my wisdom and advice. Other readers can also give you feedback before you take a cover into final production.

I once created a cover by myself for a parenting book. I write books about raising my children as one of my favorite niches. The cover of this book used an image of a sleeping baby that I thought was cute. I even worked from a good book cover template. Despite all my best efforts the book tanked until I changed the cover. Even with all of my experience, I don't have the skill to put it all together.

Hiring Talent

One of my friends paid over five hundred dollars for the cover of his book, but nobody reads it. The book fails the majority of the criteria I just shared with you. The cover is very cool and has an excellent artistic feel, but you cannot tell what genre the book is. The cover doesn't look anything like other covers in the space.

Spending money does not always lead to a great cover. I get all of my covers designed on Fiverr. That's a great website where people work for five dollars a task. I have a list of the cover designers that I use for my books at ServeNoMaster.com/orbit. If you use one of the designers from my list, you will end up with a good cover.

You should choose your main cover image before you send the design concept off. There are loads of stock photo sites with pictures that cost less than three dollars. Sometimes I find a great design, but the colors are all wrong. I will hire an artist to change the colors for me. Once the image is perfect, and the colors pop on my computer and my Kindle, I send that image to the cover designer.

For Serve No Master, I hired an artist to change the colors of the main image, but for this book, after loads of research, I found the amazing rocket ship that you see today. The colors were so perfect that I didn't change a thing. For my books about writing fast and reading fast, I may use the same design but change the colors to show that they are part of a series. When I write those, I might make this book three in the series, even though it's the first one I wrote.

When placing an order, you want to send your designer the cover art you want to use, links to similar book covers that you like, and the cover text. Your cover should contain your name, the title, and the subtitle.

On some occasions, a pure text cover is a great decision. Several of my covers have no image to allow for a larger title, and they sell quite well. No image on the cover is far and away better than a bad image.

If you hang around forums and social media group with other struggling authors, you will start to notice common themes amongst the covers of books that fail. One of them is a title written in cursive. I have never seen a book with cursive on the cover do well. A successful book with cursive on the cover might exist, but I've never seen it. Any text that's harder to read when small will cause you problems.

Be careful with combining multiple stock images. If you are not a master graphic artist, your merged design will be flawed. There is nothing worse than the bad green screen look you get with a poorly Photoshopped cover. With a vector image you can adjust components, but with a photograph you should always leave it to a professional.

The most egregious covers I see contain multiple unrelated images layered on top of each other by the author. When layering images, there are many rules and techniques as far as placement, lighting, and color agreement. All of my covers have a single image because I know that I have no talent in the image-layering department.

It's much better to have a simple, elegant cover with a clear message.

With most of the designers on Fiverr, you can request revisions until you are happy. If you have the budget, I suggest you hire multiple designers at once. I usually hire three designers at the same time to see what they create. With three covers to choose from, I am now looking for the best of the bunch. With only one design you are deciding if the cover is acceptable or not. This is a binary decision, and very limiting. You will end up with a better cover whenever you order several.

When I was first starting out as a writer, I barely had the budget for one cover design. I have books that have been in the top three for their categories for over a year with a single designer. But if you can afford it, getting a few choices from different artists is worth the effort.

If you need any help with your cover design, please feel free to upload to my Facebook page and you will get some honest feedback.

Stock Photos

Most of the books currently selling well on Amazon are using images from stock photo sites.

Yesterday I was doing some research and came upon a luxury concierge service. These services are very expensive and target people with trust funds, or billionaires flying around the world in private jets. At the top of the screen, there was a stock photo that I recognized because I used it in a presentation a few weeks ago. Nobody else has probably ever noticed that it was a stock photo.

I use stock photos from several different sites. Some of the designers on Fiverr include a stock photo in their design price. If you have a limited budget, hire one of these designers first. That is exactly how I started. Otherwise, there are loads of beautiful stock photo sites, and I will post links to the ones I use the most on my site.

Upgrading Stock Photos

If you are worried about other people coming out with the same cover or artistic integrity, you can hire a designer on Fiverr to use a stock image as a baseline and create something unique. You can have an original image that isn't too expensive. This is the best of both worlds.

Today I was working on the cover for my book, *20K a Day*. Since I mention the book in this book, I wanted to get the title dialed in. Speaking with my intern, I began to brainstorm a little bit. We went through ideas and images for about twenty minutes, and during that time we found some fascinating superhero stock photos.

None of these designs will make it onto the final cover of my book. I will probably alter the color schemes to match my next idea and put something like a book on the superhero's chest for their logo. This is a rough idea. I may go with a variation of the cover of the rocket ship on this book. In either case, I will hire an artist to modify the image to match the color and ideas that I have.

Sometimes you can't find that perfect stock image, and taking one that is almost good enough and improving it is often the best solution.

Kindle, CreateSpace and Audiobook

It's important to know the rules for Kindle, CreateSpace and audiobook covers. The most important thing is to use images that are 300 dpi. It's very hard to check the dpi of images. There are loads of tutorials online, but they are all very annoying. Stock images show the dpi before you download them. The sources I use always provide images that are high enough resolution.

DPI stands for dots per inch, and is a measurement of how the image will look when printed out. If your image resolution is too low, your paperback cover will look terrible. Images inside the book need to be high-resolution as well, or they start to look like old newspaper photographs.

The rules for book covers are always changing, so I'll post links to the appropriate Amazon pages for you.

For your paperback version, you will need a back cover and spine. For your audiobook version, you will need a square design instead of a rectangle. I go into more detail about audiobooks in your free gift, but trying to turn a rectangle into a square with black bars on the side doesn't work.

Authors try it all the time to save a few bucks, and it screams amateur hour. I tend to hire a professional to create the front cover of my book and then use a template to create the spine and back cover. I change the back cover of my books as more reviews come in. I like to put the best reviews on the back cover when they arrive. Depending on your skills with Photoshop, you might be able to do this as well. If not, all of the designers I recommend will offer a paperback version of your cover design.

15

START ON THE RIGHT FOOT

We spend more of our time on research than anything else when preparing a book for launch. We base our covers on the way Amazon displays them to potential customers. We base our titles on the way Amazon generates search results. The rest of our book preparation process will follow the same theme; don't try to reinvent the wheel.

Off the top of your head, you can probably name some of the contents at the front of a book, but you probably can't name all those pages or the correct order. I know that I can't. You need your title page, copyright page and then a few more pieces depending on your genre.

The front of your book is crucial on Amazon. Once someone is on your book listing page, Amazon displays a big button that says "Look Inside." Many potential customers will click this to get a feel for your writing style and a sneak peak at your table of contents. Later on, I will discuss where to place a free gift in your book, and how it can turn a book into a business.

For many of my books, I put the free gift at the very start, and people can see the "secret link" without actually buying the book. That's fine. When someone gives you their email address, you get to communicate with them multiple times and open a real dialog. Contact details are very powerful, so don't worry about people "stealing" from you. If someone gets your free gift without buying your book, you will make back your money tenfold.

Everything about the first ten percent of your book needs to be correctly formatted and look as professional as possible. People go through a series of steps before they make the purchasing decision, and we want to do our best to manage each phase.

If people see a cover they like, they will read your title and then click on your listing. Once on the listing, people will do a quick peek at the description to be sure the book is on the right topic; then they will scroll down to the reviews to see what the top reviewer has to say. Then they might scroll back up for a deeper read of your description, they might go read your worst review, or they might go up to the Look Inside area. Each of these is important, and we want to do our best to convert this visitor into a buyer at each off these waypoints.

Sell Your Book

When you go to a bookstore, you can pick up the book and hold it in your hands. Hardcover books have the inside and back flap to tell you about the author and a little about the story. We flip the book over to see the back cover and get a look at the author. Does the author look like other writers you enjoy?

Some people go beyond this and read the first few pages of a book before taking it to the register. The first chapter should be as enticing as possible. Do you remember how this book started? Rather than loading up the front of the book with prologues, free gifts and acknowledgments we dove right into my rejection in New York. This is an engaging story, and most people want to see how that story ends.

It's a true story, and one I usually don't tell people because it's painful. That agent hurt my feelings. The first page is designed to pull you into the story and also to catch people doing that test read before they make a buying decision.

There are sure signs that a movie will be bad, and one of them is a long scroll of title cards explaining the universe of the film. How many great movies can you think of that started with a lengthy exposition? This content is informative but not engaging.

One of the science-fiction authors that I like starts his books with a huge list of characters, their affiliations and their ranks. As a reader, I skip over these sections. This material might be valuable, but it's far better at the back of your book. No potential reader will decide they like this list of characters and then buy.

If you are creating a series of books, the challenge lies with new versus old customers. How do you get people up to speed if they haven't read the first four books in your series? Some people will read the books in your series months or years apart as you write them. When I read a series in a row, I hate that explanation of the previous book, but when have forgotten the last book, I want that explanation.

With me as a reader, it seems like you just can't win.

With Kindle, you can place clickable links inside your book that lead to other sections and your reference pages. Instead of opening your book with a dry retelling of the previous books that will bore potential readers and annoy your most ardent fans, simply place a link on the first page to your background section.

Write that story breakdown and place it in the back of your book. People that need it will click the link for a quick refresher, and people that don't can get into the meat of your book. Potential readers will be grabbed by the start of your adventure rather than get stuck reading about a different book.

Capture the Lead

No matter what genre you write in, you want to develop a relationship with your readers. Whether you are writing romance, children's books or non-fiction, a free gift will entice readers to share their email address with you. When someone reads your book, you have their attention just once.

After they finish the book, they forget you exist until Amazon shows them your next book. With an email address, you can build on the relationship and expand into something wonderful. You may have noticed that I offered a great free gift at the start of this book and have offered a few extra reasons to grab it, including access to my personal email address and the ability to ask me questions directly.

I generate a lot of content on my website. I record five podcast episodes a week, write multiple blog posts, and several informative newsletters. If I can get you to engage me through my website, I can deepen and expand our relationship. I don't want you to read this book, try to publish a book on your own, and then suffer from frustration. I want you to succeed with your book launch. A big part of that comes from feedback and having a resource you can communicate with.

Most people reading this section assume that if they send me an email, I won't ever reply to them. That they aren't unique enough, or their question isn't valuable enough to merit my attention. For this reason, a very small percentage of the people who want to ask me questions actually do. If you write me, I will respond and support you and help you to succeed.

When you have the ability to contact your readers you can turn your book into a business. You can ask them to review your next book before you release it. You can get reviews and testimonials. You can encourage them to engage with you on your blog and social media profiles. You can announce your next book when it launches to hit the ground running when it goes live. You can recommend products, services or advanced training that will fit their needs.

You can't put every single thing into one book. This book is going to end up twice my original target size. But it's still just the tip of the iceberg. My advanced bestseller coaching program contains more than one hundred hours of training and walkthrough videos. That entire course is delivered via video training so that I can go much further in-depth.

When you have a stronger connection with your audience, you can take them along the path from your book all the way to your more expensive courses, training and products. The relationship allows you to expand your offerings. You don't need my top course to launch your first book and make a nice profit, so don't worry about the hard sell. That's only for people that want to talk to me on the phone once a week and get much deeper coaching. This book has everything you need to launch your first book without needing anything else.

Your free gift should be enticing and offer real value. Adding an entire audiobook section to this book would increase the length by around thirty percent. I prefer to teach how to set up audiobooks with video or a PDF with a lot of screenshots, so delivering that content in another medium makes sense. If you grab that document, you will boost your book profits by around thirty percent every month. I think that's a pretty good value.

Do not give away garbage with your book. It's insulting to the reader. Don't buy material from somewhere else. If possible, the free gift should be worth more than the book. One of my books comes with soothing music as the free gift. The soothing music cost me more than $50 for permission to give away. With a three-dollar book, you get music that cost more than fifty bucks. That's a pretty good value.

Resist the temptation to be stingy with your gift. This is the first step in your new relationship where you turn your reader into a fan. The more value that you give away, the better. My goal with my business is to build a tribe, not to score a quick buck. I'm looking to form relationships that last for years. I want to create as much goodwill between us as possible.

I don't care if you never buy anything else from me. You bought this book, or at least grabbed it on Kindle Unlimited. That makes you a customer. If I can turn you into a fan who listens to my podcast, reads my blog and leaves the occasional comment or review, then I have succeeded. Having a long-term relationship with people who succeed following my teaching will bring more and more people into the fold.

I realize this was a long section, but that's intentional. If you capture the lead, your income will increase at least tenfold. You can turn one dollar into ten every single time. The way I create my free gift forms allows you to request your free gift without having to walk over to your laptop or pull your phone out of your pocket. You can use HTML to create a form that works inside of a Kindle. If you clicked my button earlier, you might have noticed this magic.

That's impossible to teach without some screenshots and a demo video. If you take my free gift, I'll throw in my PDF walkthrough for creating the free gift code inside your book. It will double or triple the number of people who join your mailing list over forcing them to open up a second device.

16

THE ENDING IS THE MOST IMPORTANT PART

Many people treat the end of their book like a dirty toilet. They throw some disorganized junk in there and don't care how it ends.

Your readers will never love you more than in the first few seconds after they finish your book. This is the moment when you can guide them on the course you desire.

The end of the book is vital. There is a straightforward and powerful structure to follow.

Get that Email

You can start by offering a free gift or another reward at this point. If your book is fiction, then grabbing that lead at the end of the book will work better. Right after the reader hits the cliffhanger, offer them a free short story in the continuing adventures of your main character.

Create a story that occurs before the first book or in between books one and two in your series. You can engage with your readers and let them know each time a new book in the series comes out.

Many people ignore the free gift at the start of the book. If you format incorrectly, Kindle will automatically skip your free gift page and never even show it to your readers! As a reader, you may decide that you have no interest in a free gift from an author until you see if they are any good. Who wants a free gift from a book that stinks?

Giving people a second chance to take action after they have seen the content you can deliver will allow you to build a relationship with this larger group. These people will be your biggest fans. You turned them from skeptics into believers.

Share Your Life

You need an author page with links to all of your social media profiles. Ideally, these links will all use the same naming convention. If you search for "Serve No Master" online, you will find my blog, podcast and all my social media profiles on the first page. Consistency makes it easier to engage with your readers.

We started off creating your website and social media names to prepare for this point in the book. You may have noticed that my social media content is connected to my brand, not my name. My name is extremely common. There are other Jonathan Greens out there who are far more successful and talented than I am. Having people search for me in an ocean of people with the same name is annoying. Just getting a friend to find me on social media by searching my name doesn't work.

Additionally, this is a core brand for me. I create books, products, podcasts and more under this brand. It's memorable and catchy. For my pen names, I simply use their author name for everything. If you want to create an entire brand around a pen name, that's viable. It just takes a little more work at the front to put everything together.

What Else You Got?

You also want a page with pictures of other books that you have written. Let your reader know that there is more waiting for them and they don't have to wait for your next release; it's already here.

Some people fill the back of their books with reviews and testimonials. I'm not a big fan of this personally. If someone has reached the end of your book, you don't need to tell them how great it is. They already know if they liked it. Reviews and testimonials are useful before someone buys your book, not after they read it.

A really smart move is to include the first chapter in your next book. This will increase the odds of them purchasing and reading the next book in your series. The more reasons you give the reader to stay engaged with your books the better.

Get Reviews

The final experience of your book in Kindle is crucial. The very last step is to appeal to your readers to leave a review or at least a rating. As an up-and-coming author, you know how tough it is to get reviews. I'm going to share a few of my most powerful techniques later in this book, but getting readers to take action at this point is crucial.

Some authors write a very long appeal and encourage the readers to fire up their computer, head over to Amazon, find their book listing and then post a review. This process takes far too many steps, and nobody liked your book THAT much.

At the end of a Kindle book, Amazon displays a very special page. The contents of that page can make or break you as an author. At the top of the page, there are five empty stars. If you can get a reader to simply click the fifth star before leaving your book behind, you will fly up the rankings.

Asking people for an easy action will get you much better results than asking for a difficult one. Once someone has left the star rating, it is much easier to later get them to write a deeper review, and I'll show you how to do that later.

For now, you want to end your book with an appeal for your readers to give you that crucial five-star rating.

17

TOOLS OF THE TRADE - FORMATTING

There are hundreds of schools of thought on formatting your book for Amazon. I'm not an expert on every single method, but I have tested many different methods and found the process that works the best for me. I use a Mac for all of my work, so some of my software is Mac-only. On my website, I have some walkthroughs from one of my assistants who uses a PC, showing how to format on PC as well.

There are loads of tools out there that I find difficult to use or overly complicated. You may find that you prefer a different workflow, but these are the tools and the process that I use when formatting my books.

Vellum

My favorite formatting tool is Vellum. I can import my book into Vellum after the editing process is complete. The organization is simply beautiful, and it's so easy to make any necessary changes. I can drag and drop sections to move around the order as needed. The software provides a preview of every different Kindle model, so you can see how your book will look to your customers.

Eventually you are going to release bundles and collections of your books as a revenue booster. When that times comes, Vellum is a dream come true. You can drag pages between different projects. Assembling and formatting your collection will take only five minutes. Once you create the perfect author page with your social media links, you can just drag it into your other books.

Vellum exports into multiple formats, and I love it. It is how I will format this book and all my other books for the foreseeable future. As of now, this software is Mac-only, but perhaps in the future they will release a PC version.

I have used a lot of other formatting tools in the past, but I have already taken all my older books and reformatted them using Vellum.

My favorite thing about Vellum is the development team. When I first used the software, it couldn't format bullet points. If you had bullet points in your original document, you could copy and paste them into Vellum, but there was nothing native. I emailed support and within a few weeks, they pushed out an update that included incredible native bullet points.

Very rarely does a software developer respond so quickly. It's nice knowing that any changes or ideas I have in the future will get added to the software.

You can play around with the program for free.

The pricing structure is a little strange. You don't pay until you export your book into the Amazon-friendly format.

It's thirty bucks to export one book, a hundred bucks for a pack of ten, or two hundred bucks for unlimited. Releasing books is my business, and that two hundred dollars has saved me hours and hours of work and stress. There are ways to format your book without spending any money, but I find them challenging.

Scrivener

I love Scrivener. There are loads of authors who swear by Scrivener's ebook export option. You can bypass the need for Vellum and have Scrivener output a file in the correct format for Amazon. I don't know if I'm just missing something, but my exports from Scrivener always have problems. They are usually ninety percent of what I want, but then I still need to go in and clean up things.

There are loads of great exporting tutorials online, and I have tried to follow them, but I just couldn't get it quite right. For me, the final presentation is everything, and I find exporting from Scrivener directly into an ebook format too difficult.

I have recently switched to using Scrivener exports to create my paperback version, however. For a very long time, I copied each chapter from Scrivener into a Word template. It was a tedious process but generated professional quality books. Recently, I start exporting from Scrivener using a particular paperback book formula. I'll have to show you on my website because there are a bunch of key little steps in the process that require screenshots or a video walkthrough. If you miss one checkbox, your export will be unusable.

I export into Word format and do my final editing in Word. Once the Word formatting is perfect, I will save as a PDF and upload that to CreateSpace for my final version.

If you purchase only one tool from everything I mention in this book, go for Scrivener. The developers don't have an affiliate program, so I don't get a penny for the recommendation. But it's the ultimate workhorse. You can learn to format your books into any format you need using this tool. It just takes a little work to learn the process.

Calibre

Calibre is another excellent formatting tool. This tool is free, it's open-source, and it's updated several times a week. I used Calibre to format my very first book, and I have some walkthroughs that I will email you showing how to use this tool to format.

I mainly use it to convert books between multiple formats, from EPUB to PDF to MOBI and back. It's very powerful and can generate the final file you will upload to Amazon. I would love to share a more extensive explanation with you here, but I don't want to be disingenuous. I haven't formatted a book with Calibre in a very long time.

Formatting a book with Calibre is a little harder than Vellum, but you may find it easier than going straight from Scrivener.

Calibre works on both Mac, PC, and Linux.

18

FORMATTING FOR KINDLE

K nowing the correct formats to upload is very important. When I first started working with Amazon, I was very frustrated and considered the formatting part of the process the most daunting.

It doesn't have to be hard. Once you know what Amazon wants, the process is quite smooth.

You cannot upload a .docx Word document to Amazon. The format is not compatible with the Kindle software. You need to generate a .mobi, .epub, or a .zip file. Those are the two formats that work best and will give you a great-looking book.

I currently upload my books to Amazon's Kindle platform using .mobi exports from Vellum, but in the past I uploaded many books using the .zip format. Both will maintain your book structure and look great when you check in the Kindle preview tool.

Pay Someone

You can always pay someone else to format your book. With most people you pay to format your book, they will give you back an uneditable version. I hate this. You write your book, pay someone to format it for you and then you launch the book. A week later you get an email pointing out a single typo. If you want to correct that typo, you have to correct your copy of the book and then send that file to the formatter and pay them all over again.

The last time I tried to hire a formatter, it ended with me in a rage and a full refund. He made some mistakes in the formatting and demanded that I pay double to fix them. He could have simply emailed me the editable file to let me fix it myself, but he refused to do that.

I do use professionals when I want to upload a book to Smashwords. That's where you upload a book that you want to be permanently free. Their formatting algorithm is baffling to me. So, I hire a professional.

My books are fluid and change over time. I will update this book dozens of times over the next ten years as technology changes and Amazon adapts. I want to keep this book relevant. Paying someone else every single time I want to update or make a small change is a nightmare. The cost would become prohibitive, and I don't want to have any factor weighing against giving my readers the best experience possible.

There are full-service companies that target new authors. They charge from a few hundred to a few thousand bucks. Some of them even take a percentage of your sales revenue. As far as I'm concerned, they're gouging every single person.

If you really can't handle formatting yourself, hire someone on Fiverr to do it rather than dealing with one of these nightmare houses. They will charge you hundreds of dollars for ten bucks of work, and their final product is never that great.

I know this is a burgeoning industry, but so far nothing I have seen has impressed me. Offering to format your book and then upload it for you is ridiculous. You can learn how to do all of this in less than an hour. It's not worth throwing away hundreds of dollars that would be far better spent on marketing campaigns later on.

19

FORMATTING FOR CREATESPACE

For CreateSpace, where you will upload your paperback version, you can upload a Word file. The problem is the way Word files are formatted. They depend on the fonts inside of the recipient's computer. If your book uses a font that is not native inside CreateSpace, your upload will look weird. It is better to convert your book into a PDF format and upload that to CreateSpace. Your fonts will be preserved, and the book will look as you intended.

I always upload in PDF format so that my fonts are locked in and my positioning cannot be changed. If the program misreads your Word file, you can end up with a page count shift. Just moving one sentence from page seven to the top of page eight can cause a domino effect that turns your entire book into a train wreck. Word has a save as PDF option, so there is no reason not to do it.

Scrivener Export

Right now I export the final edit of my book using the "paperback compiler" tool inside of Scrivener. I export into Word format rather than PDF, however. I always find that something went wrong in the export and that I want to make some changes before the book is perfect in my eyes. Usually I do something wrong with the page numbers, the headings or the footers. I also prefer to build my table of contents inside of Word.

These are probably problems that are unique to me, but I want to be fully transparent with you. You can master the Scrivener export and push out a PDF directly without needing Word. I'm just not at that level yet. I like doing my final little tweaks in Word.

Before you can export from Scrivener, you have to start setting up your book in CreateSpace. Amazon allows you to choose different book sizes. A book that is 5x8 inches will be different from a book that is 6x9 inches; the pages will be different sizes. Once you know your final trim size, you can tell Scrivener to export the correct dimensions.

I like this process, and it's the fastest way I know to prep a book for CreateSpace.

Resolution Requirements

I mentioned it earlier, but it bears repeating. Your images for Create-Space must be 300 dpi, or they will look terrible in your printed book. Most images for the web are only 72 dpi.

When you upload a book with inferior images, CreateSpace will yell at you. You can expect a lot of warnings and flashing red exclamation points. If you try and push your book through despite these warnings, their manual reviewer might still stop your book.

Here is the best way to increase the dpi of an image: get the largest version of the image you can find, place it inside your book in Word, and then shrink it by dragging on the corners. As you shrink the image, the dpi increases. If you want to get more technical, head over to my website.

ISBN

Do not pay for an ISBN. This is another scam that people fall into, and they pay anywhere from ten to hundreds of dollars for one of these numbers. Amazon will give you a free one during the Create-Space upload process. There is absolutely no benefit to getting your ISBN from another source.

Interior Template

Once you pick the trim size for your book, you can download a template for your final book file. I used these templates for a very long time and only recently switched to using Scrivener export. Amazon will provide a ten-chapter Word file with demo filler placed into each chapter.

This makes it very easy to copy and paste each chapter into your book without messing up the formatting. If you are having trouble with the other formatting methods, this is the easiest and cheapest way to do it. You don't need any technical expertise.

When you copy in your text, make sure you use "copy and match formatting." This will convert your text into the font and size of the template.

Cover Template

I order my first cover designs long before I finish writing the book itself. I have already received the first three designs for the cover of this book and requested some revisions to get to that perfect final version that you saw before you made your purchase.

When you create a physical book, the page count determines the thickness of your book. The spine of your book gets bigger as the book gets longer. If you don't know the page count, then you don't know how thick your spine will be, and therefore you can't create the cover yet.

Once you have your front cover, you can wait on formatting your final CreateSpace cover until you have finished and uploaded the interior content.

Amazon generates a new template size for every additional twenty pages in your book. A book with twenty pages gets the same templates as a book with thirty-nine, but at forty you get a new template.

Creating Your CreateSpace Cover

There are two main ways to generate your CreateSpace cover: you can pay your Fiverr designer a few extra bucks, or you can do it yourself. I tend to do it myself because I like to make additional changes down the line.

You take the appropriately sized cover template from CreateSpace and open it with Photoshop or Affinity. Take the cover for your Kindle book and drag it over the front cover spot in the template. You may have to resize it a little bit, but the dimensions will match.

Now you just need to add your spine and back cover. You can either use a template or create these parts from scratch.

As an additional bonus for joining my mailing list, I will send you $67 worth of templates that I paid extra for the rights to. These are the EXACT templates I use to make my paperback covers.

The Uploading Process

Uploading a book to CreateSpace is confusing. You may have noticed that many independent authors only have a digital version of their book. They are intimated by the paperback process, don't think they will make sales anyway, and then leave a great deal of money on the table.

Follow these steps in the correct order and your process will be okay.

Before you format your book for paperback, log into the CreateSpace website and start your project. Submit the title and author information. During this process, it will ask you if you have your own ISBN number, want to buy one, or would like a free one. Take the free one.

Then you save and stop this process. Go back to your book and format everything. The book itself needs to contain that ISBN on the copyright page. This is one of the reasons I hate hiring someone else to format my book. If I want to add the ISBN, I have to pay him again.

You can format your book using any method that works for you. You can simply download the template from CreateSpace that matches your book dimensions and copy each chapter into it. That is how the majority of my books were formatted.

Once you have your final interior book content formatted, go back to CreateSpace and upload your interior file. You may have to go back and forth making a few final edits before your interior is ready for primetime. I always catch little mistakes when checking my work in the CreateSpace previewer.

Once your interior is perfect, CreateSpace will give you a final page count. You can download a template with the correct spine size and cover dimensions. Create your paperback cover yourself or get your designer to create the final paperback cover for you.

Upload your final cover design and submit to the manual review process. A real person will look at your formatting before they approve your book to go live.

This process can seem complicated because you go back and forth a few times, but if you follow these simple steps, it is very achievable. As always if you get stuck, check my blog for detailed walkthroughs, or just reply to one of my emails and I'll get you unstuck.

20

TURN YOUR LISTING INTO A SALES MACHINE

The description section is not where you tell people what your book is all about. It's not where you introduce yourself or explain the outline of your story.

Each component of your book can only serve a single purpose. The cover gets people to visit your listing page. We must remain laser-focused.

The description is to convince people to buy and read your book. Any other goal will lower your sales numbers and limit your potential for success.

Most authors write their descriptions as a summary of the book: a bird's eye view of the story or topic that the book will discuss. But this does not increase their sales numbers.

There is a big difference between content writing and copywriting. Copywriting is an entirely different art form; that's why it will be covered in a separate book.

Don't fall into the common trap of writing a dull or descriptive summary of your book. Don't list the topics the book covers to help readers make "informed" buying decisions. There are other ways to ensure that your reader knows what they are buying. This section is there to get them excited about your book and bring them across the finish line.

Sell Your Book

Your book page on Amazon is a sales page. It is the infomercial for your book. Do not think of Amazon as a big book catalog that lists titles in alphabetical order. It's a dynamic system that rewards the strong and punishes the weak.

With a novel, get your reader excited about where the story is going. Don't waste time explaining the backstory or the world the characters inhabit. Do not tell me what happens, show me.

With a non-fiction book, you want to follow the traditional copy-writing process. Point out the problem, explain how your book solves the problem, and show them what life will be like after they read your book.

Take a look at the books in your category that are selling and those that are failing. You will find that the better books also have better descriptions. You want to intrigue and entice your visitors. Make them yearn to read your book to find out what happens next or to solve their problem.

Weave a story that your reader will want to be a part of. Engage their imagination and guide them to clicking that "add to cart" button.

I have several extensive blog posts on my site that detail the copy-writing process if you want to continue to grow and master this craft. For now, start by modeling the structure of the books in your space that are doing well.

Formatting

Amazon allows you to use HTML in your descriptions. You can make sentences big or small. You can create bullet points and break lines. You can create words that are bold, underlined or in italics.

Your book description is a canvas, and these advanced constructions are the paint. Take the time to create a beautiful description and you will move a lot more books.

Your first description will have mistakes in it. Learning HTML is hard and even when it looks perfect on your computer, you will find some mistakes when you publish the description on Amazon. Many authors ignore their actual listing and never notice that there are big spaces between some paragraphs and tiny ones between others.

You don't have to learn HTML or go to computer school to master this process. You should have already set up your author blog and installed WordPress by now. WordPress is my preferred blogging platform, and I have loads of tutorials on my site if you need them.

Open up a new blog post and write your description there. You can save the post as a draft while you work on it. Using the list of allowed HTML tags from Amazon's website, create a listing that looks perfect. Once you are satisfied with the artistry of your listing, click on the little button that says "source." This will show you the HTML version of your blog post.

Simply copy and paste that into the Kindle publishing platform. Depending on how fast Amazon moves, your description will appear in six to forty-eight hours. Once that new description is up, take a look and adjust anything that looks weird.

Amazon formats HTML in its own way, so it will look different from any tool you test with. That's fine. The beauty of the system is how quickly you can make changes to get everything perfect.

There are a lot of tools out there that promise to help you write great descriptions and format them to perfection, but none of them have ever impressed me. Doing it for free using Wordpress is the fastest, easiest and cheapest way to create a perfectly formatted description.

Author Central

Once your book is live, you can create an Author Central account, where you can upload your author photo, create a biography and link to some of your social media. Amazon is always changing the integrations. For a while, you could connect to Twitter and YouTube accounts, but then you couldn't.

Right now you can link to your blog posts, and you have to upload any videos directly to Amazon. In your author biography, you can encourage people to follow you on Amazon, read your blog or visit you on social media. We will go deeper into perfecting your Author Central profile shortly.

One thing that many authors miss is the advanced listing editing tools inside Author Central. When you log in for the first time, you will need to claim your book and confirm that you are the author. Once you have connected the book to your author profile, you can add some advanced sales content to your listing.

You can add a few special sections:
• Editorial Reviews
• From the Author
• From the Inside Flap
• From the Back Cover
• About the Author

As you get great reviews, you can add the best ones to your editorial reviews section. When you add solid content to each of these sections, your book stops looking like a self-published book and starts to look very professional.

You should continue to tweak and improve your listing for the months and years after you initially release it. I rewrite all my book descriptions at least once a year and add additional content far more often.

Using these additional sections will help your book to slide to the top of the rankings and push down the competitors that leave these sections blank.

21

THE SECRET TO GOLDEN CATEGORIES

P utting your book in the wrong category can end the game before it even gets started.

Some people slip books into the wrong categories for strategic reasons. Every time I look for science-fiction novels, there are loads of inappropriate erotica books shoved into the listings. Amazon will eventually course-correct and shut down all the books playing that game.

Your book answers a specific question. It is designed and written for a very specific reader. Understanding how that reader peruses Amazon and makes buying decisions is the first step on the path to making that sale. For non-fiction books, many people type in the name of their problem and use the search results. This is how people shop for books about writing fast, quitting their job or learning how to cut their hair.

You will make a lot of sales from category listings, but your keywords will often generate the majority of your sales.

With fiction books, nearly all of your sales will come from being in the correct categories. When was the last time you typed "dragon book" into Amazon? That's not how we approach fiction. When searching for a fiction book at the bookstore we go to the section we like. I walk to the science fiction section and then start looking around.

I shop on Amazon the same way. When I am looking for a new book to read, I go to the science fiction section, limit to books released in the past thirty days and then sort by popularity. This is how I find new books that are also readable. Your average Amazon reader is sophisticated and searches in a similar way.

If you put your hard-boiled detective novel in the police procedural category, your audience won't find you. If you put your book on curing tinnitus in the social sciences section, your book will die a lonely death.

Researching and analyzing categories is just as important as researching keywords. For some books, eighty percent or more of your sales will come from your category. This is imperative.

Amazon is a living beast and cannot be treated like the Dewey Decimal System. This is not a card catalog, but a dynamic shopping system. The purpose of Amazon is to sell product. That is the single goal of Amazon. Amazon wants to help your reader find the best book for them. When Amazon brings a reader to the right book, that person buys the book, and Amazon makes money.

The categories in Amazon are updated all the time. If I included a comprehensive listing of every category on Amazon right now, by the time this book is published that list will be incorrect. You should check and update your categories at least every three months to stay on top of Amazon.

Taking action to improve your listing and adapt to Amazon's changing platform is how you can maintain sales for years after you publish a book.

Easy Category

Amazon allows you to place your book in two categories for Kindle, two categories for paperback and then at least one more for your audiobook version. Let's start with choosing two Kindle categories.

You want to use your categories as a one-two punch to drive sales.

The first category should be easier to rank for. I love finding a category where the top book is ranked around #15,000 in the overall Amazon rankings. I know that my book can beat that. When my book becomes number one in this category, Amazon will add "Bestseller" to my book when it appears in search results.

This bestseller status will increase sales and help to drive me up to the top of my harder category.

Some people like to use inappropriate categories to "game the system." That's stupid and has no longevity. Would you be impressed if this book was #1 in the microscopes category? Your easier category still has to be relevant and valuable.

If you choose a category that your book doesn't fit in, you might get a bestseller star, but your sales won't increase. I want to get a sale from everyone visiting the easier category. I want every single person who visits that category to buy my book and boost my rankings.

When you begin your category research, you may find that there are a few categories that would fit the book you are writing. This book could be any of these categories:

- Business writing
- Authorship
- Creativity
- Home-Based Business
- Communications
- Direct Marketing
- Writing Skills

This book would make sense in any of those categories. From them and some deeper research, I will choose the easiest one to rank for as my crutch.

When selecting categories, your easy pick should be one that is relevant.

Tough Category

For your tough category, find one that is a little harder than your first category. I like to use twelve thousand as my baseline. With my system, I know I can get any book to around that ranking pretty easily.

If the bestseller in my easier category is around #15,000, then I know I can get to bestseller status. For the stronger category, I like to ensure that I can rank somewhere in the top twenty. If the twentieth book is ranked around #20,000, I am happy. I want my book to be number one in the easy category and on the first page with my hard category.

The first category is for ranking and to generate some momentum; the harder category will have a lot more traffic and visitors. Placement in this category will generate more revenue for me.

With your category placement, you want to be strategic.

Secret Categories

When you go to upload your book to Kindle, you may find that the category you want isn't there. Your perfect category is missing from the options!

Amazon updates their public system far more often than their backend. When your preferred category is missing, don't just select a similar one as this can mess up your progress. Just choose one category and leave the other one blank.

Once your book is live, you can email Kindle Support, and they will manually add you to the better category. This is a serious competitive advantage for you. Many authors limit themselves to the incomplete list, and you can dominate a better category simply because the competition doesn't know about it.

Amazon is always changing categories around, and you will sometimes find a new category that much better fits the problem you solve. With non-fiction, Amazon will release a new category that perfectly matches your book.

Right now your book is in the auditory problems category, and that's pretty good. But then Amazon opens up a category called "tinnitus." Manually moving your tinnitus book into the better category will spike your sales and give you a lot more authority.

Jack Rabbit

Sometimes you will notice your book drifting down the rankings. This drop can happen after an initial barrage of sales if you don't receive enough reviews. Amazon will start to slide you down.

You might have a book right now ranked in the hundred thousands or millions. That book is not dead. Changing categories can bring you back into the game. Amazon will often give you a second chance when you change categories.

There are always several categories that would be a great fit for your book. Moving your book between categories every few months will keep the book fresh. You will also go in front of a whole new audience. The people who read books on authorship are not the same people who read books on working from home.

Hopping between categories will expand your audience reach.

When you are running a promotion, as we'll discuss in a moment, you may drive tens of thousands of downloads for your book in a single day. When I launched Serve No Master, I ran a one-day promotion and became the 2nd best free book on all of Amazon. I was #1 in any category where I placed my book.

When you are running a promotion with a lot of external traffic, whether paid or free downloads, changing your categories throughout the day will do something magical. You can switch categories and become number one in four categories instead of just two.

These rankings won't last forever, but your book will have credibility in more categories. Again, don't put your book in wrong categories just to mess with rankings, but switching to a relevant category mid-promotion can magnify the benefits of that promotion.

22

SELL BOOKS OR MAKE MONEY

It is time to price your book, and this is a daunting decision. The price of your book will dramatically affect how much money you make and how Amazon markets your book.

You can release a book on Kindle to drive people into your more expensive course. If this is your goal, a lower price point makes sense. When you make your money after the initial sale, then you want to move as many books as possible.

At 99 cents you might move twenty books a day, instead of just ten books at $2.99. You don't care about your Amazon paycheck. You are building a list from your book, and it's a loss leader. Many businesses operate this way. Most video game consoles are sold at a loss. They lose money on that machine because they know they will make the money back on video game purchases.

If you are just starting out and don't have a backend in place, a higher price point makes more sense for you. Your primary revenue will come from Amazon directly. Eventually you will build out your business infrastructure, but for now you want to generate maximum revenue.

If your only goal is to get books out there, consider making the book permanently free. It's much easier to rank a free book and find new readers. If you are a fiction author, having a free book to start your series is an excellent way to capture readers that end up paying for the next twenty books. The free sample is a classic and effective sales technique.

Different Royalties

The pricing of your book will dramatically change your royalties. Amazon pays royalties in two bands: thirty percent and seventy percent. When your book is listed at $2.98 or below, Amazon only pays you 30% of each sale. For a 99-cent book, you will get around thirty cents a sale.

Between $2.99 and $9.99, Amazon bumps you up to 70%. With a book listed at $2.99, you get about two bucks a sale.

I would love to predict your exact commission, but it fluctuates for every book. The size of your book file will affect commissions. If your book is full of high-definition images, Amazon will charge you a high transfer fee and your final commission will be lower.

Pay close attention to your royalty band when pricing your book.

Pricing Phases

Your Kindle book will go through different pricing phases when you launch. When I first publish my book to Amazon, I price it at 99 cents. I then reach out to as many reviewers as I can. I send out loads of gift copies, and Amazon charges me a buck for each one. We'll cover why this phase is so critical in the Launch and Reviews sections.

Once your book has enough reviews to generate some traction, it is time to plan a free promotion. The free promotion should only last one or two days, and it's a chance to get eyeballs on your book. During this promotion, you will get tons of downloads and introduce new people to you as an author.

When the promotion ends, your book will shoot up the paid

rankings for a little while. Your book should be 99 cents for a few days to generate as many sales as possible.

Once this process is complete, you can settle on your final book price and stay there. You will only adjust pricing again when you run another promotion.

Format Prices

Royalties are very different on each platform. Kindle royalties are mainly based on the size of the file you upload. For Kindle Unlimited, longer books pay out more. You get paid around half a penny for each page anyone reads from your book in this program.

With CreateSpace, where I publish all my paperbacks, the pricing is very different. Physical books exist in the real world. There is a cost to turning on the machine, printing the pages, and shipping the book out to a customer. The printing options you choose will affect your royalty.

It costs more money to print pages in color, and choosing that option can slice your royalty to the bone. One of my friends accidentally chose color for a black and white book and lost about eighty percent of his paycheck. One little mistake dramatically hurt his bank account.

When you upload your book to Createspace, you can choose the type of paper you want and if the cover should be glossy. Fancier features and larger trim sizes increase the printing cost and decrease your royalty. In general, your paperback royalty will be in the thirty to forty percent range.

For your average book, the printing costs will be three to four bucks. If you try to price the paperback at $2.99, Amazon will lose money on every single sale. Even if they kept all of the money, the printing itself costs more than that.

Createspace won't let you sell your book at a loss. The software will automatically stop you when you try. You can price your book low enough to knock your commission to zero if you really want to. But you don't.

You want to price the paperback at a cost that makes sense and makes the Kindle book more enticing. As a rule of thumb, price your book at $7.99 or $8.99 to get started. This is a rough guideline and if you feel stuck, reply to one of my emails.

Pricing By Country

Your book will be a different price on each of the Amazon's platforms. If you were so inclined, you could manually control the price of your book in every country where Amazon has a presence.

This is a lot of extra work. Just let Amazon price match across platforms. This is much easier, and it's fair for your customers. Everyone pays the same cost no matter where they live. If you want to lower the price in a particular country for a specific reason, you can.

Don't bother lowering the price in one country in the hopes of spiking sales in another. Each Amazon is a unique business, and there are firewalls between them. Each month you will get a direct deposit from a dozen different Amazons. Each country will pay you separately.

Amazon Recommends

Amazon has a very helpful tool when pricing your book. They will tell you the price that will generate the most sales and the price that will generate the most revenue. The tool is not perfect, but it is quite helpful as a guideline.

I use it for some of my books, and I ignore it for others. It's really up to you to play around with pricing and see how smart Amazon is. Like Grammarly, the software inside of Amazon is on the path to achieving sentience, but it isn't quite there yet.

23

BECOME A RESPECTED AMAZON AUTHOR

Whether you use your real name or create a pen name, you need to create a customer-facing identity. You don't want to share every aspect of your personality and life with your audience. If I told you my position on political issues right now, I would alienate many readers. I don't write political books, so injecting politics into my author identity doesn't make sense.

There are many people with the same name as me. My name is not nearly enough information to make me unique or memorable in your mind.

There are parts of my life and personality that end up in my books and public-facing social media.

You want to create a solid idea of who your author is, what customers like about that identity, and what pieces of information you should share. You don't want to use any personal social media accounts as an author. If you use a profile to connect with customers that already connects to all of your real friends and family, you could experience some uncomfortable blow-through. Even if you want to share every single aspect of your life with your readership, you don't want to violate the privacy of the people around you.

There is nothing weirder than a fan showing up at your house or sending a friend request to one of your kids. I one time had my home address posted on a very creepy website. One of the members of that forum later murdered several people. I got very lucky, so now I also take security very seriously. If you want to know the rest of that story, listen to episode nineteen, "Dealing with Hate Mail," on my podcast.

Put together a file on your computer with the pieces of your life that you will share with the public: the author's identity kit. This folder is where you store any photos that are going to get shared across your online profiles. There is no value to having a different picture on each of your social media profiles; that will only confuse your audience.

Centralize everything to make it easier for you to remember.

Social Media Integration

You can integrate several pieces of social media with Amazon via your author page. Right now Amazon allows authors to connect a blog feed to their author profile, upload pictures and videos, write a biography, post upcoming events, and create a custom link.

Your first step is to choose a custom link that matches your author name or your brand. It takes a few hours for Amazon to confirm your link, so do this step immediately. You will want to share this link at certain points in your business development, so getting the right link set up now is important. You don't want another author with the same name grabbing the link you wanted. A big part of building a business is establishing Internet properties that sync up.

You should already have your blog set up, so connect your RSS feed to your author page. This will automatically display your latest blog posts to your audience. Now you should begin seeing how everything connects together. There is a reason you set up and started your blog before writing your book. Now those first few blog posts are invaluable. Having content that has aged a few weeks is better than five posts you write the day after launching your book. We are creating some credibility and depth to your identity.

Upload your primary author photo. Do not screw around with your author photo. Do not just use your favorite Facebook photo. People expect a certain look when they click on your author profile, and if you disappoint them you will lose sales. Do not use an amateur or silly photo. It should at least look like it was taken by a professional. With a pen name, just use a stock photo or drawing that fits your niche. If you're not sure what to do, look at the profiles of competing authors in your space, or post your picture on my Facebook wall and ask.

You can also add book trailers, other videos and more photos to your author page. It's really up to you how much you add to your page. As long as the content is professional, adding more will look good. You can get away with just one photo for now, but feel free to build up your profile over time.

The Biography

Your biography is there to excite visitors and convince them to buy more of your books. Share a few exciting parts of your history and include links to your social media profiles. You want to make it as easy as possible for people who want to connect with you to find you.

Not every one of your readers will be able to find you using search engines. Give them a link they can copy and paste to visit your blog and other social media profiles.

It takes up to twenty-four hours for updates to post to your profile. After you have submitted your profile, come back tomorrow to see how it looks to someone visiting your page.

You will notice that about halfway down the page is a "see more" button. The bottom half of your profile is hidden from casual viewers. Your links should be placed above this button, ensuring that every single visitor to your page sees them. The way things look when we submit them is often very different from what customers see.

With every step of this process, take the time to look at your profile from the customer's side. Customer experience is everything. We want to make things as easy and pleasant as possible for our readers.

Upgrade Your Book Page

After you have linked your first book to your profile, make sure that you go and upgrade the sales page for that book. As you release different formats of your book, they will connect to your author profile. You are allowed to make different changes to the listings for each format. Check out how your book page looks for the paperback, digital and audio versions.

Whenever you get a fantastic review somewhere other than Amazon, you want to share it on your book page using Author Central.

These little steps add up to build the foundation for a real business, rather than a flash in the pan book.

Upload Your Picture

Before you upload any pictures to the Internet, scrub the metadata from them. If you are using a stock image photo, that photo will have links hidden inside of it back to the original site. If you took a picture with your smartphone, it will have GPS data embedded into it. Someone could download the photo, copy and paste that number into Google Earth and have a bird's eye view of your house.

It probably won't happen, but it's better to be safe than sorry.

On Mac, there is a fabulous free program called ImageOptim. It cleans out all private data from image files and optimizes them for online display. You can drag your entire author folder into this program, and it will detect and clean up all of your photos.

On PC, you just right-click on the image and select properties. Click on the Details tab and click "remove properties and personal information."

It only takes a few seconds to scrub your files, and it is worth the effort. You probably won't have a problem if you forget this step, but it's better to do it now.

If you want to see what data is hidden in one of your photos, just right-click and select properties. You might just be surprised what information was embedded into the back of the photo.

Most social media sites and Amazon will scrub your file when you upload it, but your blog certainly won't. It's better to clear up everything now just to be on top of it.

24

HOW TO GET REVIEWS EVEN IF YOU DON'T HAVE ANY FRIENDS

The key to success within any system is to know the rules. If you tried to play rugby without knowing the rules, you would have no chance of success. Without knowing how Amazon ranks books, you will struggle to succeed.

There are three key metrics that Amazon tracks and values above all others. The first is traffic, and this is where independent authors often fail themselves. They work hard creating and crafting the perfect book. They upload the book, following all the correct steps. Then they think the work is over. Amazon will do all the work of selling their book while they kick back and relax.

After they sell ten copies to friends and family, the book drops into the dark recesses at the bottom of the Amazon rankings. They did everything right as an author but failed abysmally as a publisher.

Once you upload your book, you become the publisher. You need to make those sales happen, not just rely on Amazon. Amazon rewards those who take action, and has zero mercy for the passive.

Amazon wants you to bring visitors from other websites. The more people who visit your page directly, rather than through searches and categories, the more Amazon will love you. Traffic is a crucial metric that you don't want to skip. Don't worry; I'll show you how to get all the traffic you need in the Launch section.

The second metric that Amazon looks at is sales. This metric is about more than just total sales. Amazon cares far more about conversion.

Imagine that there are two books about curing tinnitus. They each sell ten copies a day. Book A sold ten copies, with one hundred visitors. Book A is converting at 10%. Ten percent of the people who visit the page for book A make a purchase.

Book B also sold ten copies, but this book had one thousand visitors. Both books seem great because they each sold ten copies, but book B is converting at 1%. Book A is converting ten times better.

If you could buy a lottery ticket, which one would you choose? Do you want a one percent chance of winning or ten percent?

Amazon is a business. The purpose of Amazon is to sell product. Amazon is going to actively reward book A, and book B will continue to be pushed down the rankings unless something changes. For Amazon, failure to convert is an unforgivable sin.

The third metric is reviews. This metric is harder to track because Amazon uses a very complicated algorithm. There are several factors the go into their formula: total number of reviews, age of reviews, and average review score. These factors are all based on a foundational metric. What is your review conversion percentage?

How many books do you have to sell to generate one review?

The answer to that question is the secret of the universe. You must actively do everything in your power to beg, borrow and appeal for more reviews.

The average reader has no understanding of how Amazon operates. When they see a book with loads of reviews, they assume their vote won't count, so they don't leave a review.

If your book has a thousand reviews, but none in the past year, Amazon will put your book out to pasture. The book was awesome, but its heyday is over. They will play the orchestral music and drag you off the stage.

More than anything else, once your book is live you must actively pursue reviews. Do everything you can to get more reviews. Don't do anything unethical, but you must actively pursue reviews on a continual basis.

White Hat Black Hat

Let me be very clear here. Amazon has zero mercy for people caught breaking the rules. One of the guys in my original mastermind, when I was learning the Kindle system, got caught. He was messing around with reviews and the Kindle Unlimited system.

I didn't ask him exactly what he was doing. As soon as he told me that one sentence, I knew he was banned for life. He's back working in a cubicle now.

Do not pay for reviews or get suckered in by sketchy review services.

Amazon's central server is close to achieving full sentience. Amazon tracks every single thing you do on the site. Amazon tracks IPs, drops cookies, and tracks locations. If you logged into Amazon once from your cousin's computer ten years ago, Amazon still knows.

Read Amazon's rules and abide by them. It's fine to solicit reviews from readers and give away copies in exchange for reviews, but it's not ok to pay for reviews. Never accept or solicit reviews from someone who hasn't read your book. That stuff is garbage. Don't waste your time playing that silly game.

Turn Readers into Reviewers

Your first task is to improve your reader-to-reviewer ratio. Do everything in your power to remind your readers that you need reviews. If you can convey the importance of reviews to your audience, more of them will take action. Seeking out external reviewers and sending out copies is fine when you are first launching, but you want to set processes in place now to generate reviews over time.

End of Book

The final page of your book should be an appeal for a rating. When someone is reading a book on their Kindle, asking them to fire up the computer to leave you a review is too much. Very few people will do it.

Instead, ask them to rate the book. They can just click on one to five stars to rate your book without leaving their Kindle. These ratings aren't as good as reviews, but they are WAY better than nothing. If you can get a reader to rate your book, you are on the first step to succeeding. You have convinced your reader to take an action.

Email List

Do everything in your power to get readers onto your email list. Offer them amazing free gifts and additional information. You don't need to sell them anything to grow your business. I'm giving away as much content as I can to anyone who gives me their email address. I don't have any downline product to sell to my readers.

I want that email address so that I can build the relationship and use that opportunity to ask for an honest review. If someone left a star rating, it's much easier for them to write out a full review beneath that rating. Amazon stores all the data to make it easy for people to upgrade and edit their reviews.

You should bear in mind how long it takes people to read your entire book. If you have a short book, you might send an email out after a day or two, but if your book is long you may ask for that review after a week or two.

As far as the technical process, I have some step-by-step PDFs that will walk you through setting up your email system and integrating it into your book. If you enter your email in the form at the beginning of this book, I'll mail them to you.

Amazon's Best Reviewers

Amazon treats reviewers like gladiators in an arena. Every single product on Amazon is ranked, but so are all of the reviewers. There are loads of professional reviewers.

If you get to the top echelon of reviewers, Amazon has an elite program. They send these respected reviews LOADS of cool stuff for free. The main program is called Vine Voice. These people get tens or even hundreds of thousands of dollars in free stuff, all because their reviews are trusted and respected.

Trust is the foundation of the reviewer algorithm. When someone leaves a review, other people can say it was helpful or not helpful. If you write a million reviews but consistently get downvoted, your reviewer rank will be terrible.

The quality of reviews is more important than anything else. Most people trying to move up the ranks are glad to review Kindle books to beef up their score. You can look at the top thousand reviewers directly on Amazon. Most of them have their email address listed because they like free stuff.

Find a reviewer who mostly leaves positive reviews and has reviewed a book similar to yours. Email them explaining that you saw they reviewed a similar book, and you would be honored to send them a complimentary copy of your book in exchange for an honest review.

These reviews are worth more because they are imbued with more trust. A review from a top 100 reviewer holds a lot of weight with Amazon and will also increase your sales numbers.

There are ways to automate this process using software, and I can show you how to do that on my site.

Goodreads

Goodreads is the social media platform for people who love books. Amazon now owns it. On this platform, you can find groups of readers who love getting free books and leaving reviews. This is an excellent way to find people that prefer a particular format. There are groups of people who just love free audiobooks.

Sending out loads of free copies of your book is a great way to get that initial momentum when you are a new author and don't have any following. The more time you spend on Goodreads, the more you will get dialed into the mood of the culture.

Do NOT post your book in inappropriate groups appealing for reviews. That is unacceptable over there. Only post your book in groups or threads where they are looking for books to review.

Friends and Family

Most books and courses on Kindle out there advise you to turn to friends and family for reviews. This is a risky proposition and a total waste of time. If twenty people close to you promise to leave a review, at best one of them will bother to do it.

You will have your feelings hurt, and it becomes awkward all around. You start to think that you're the only one this has happened to. Everyone else has a great social circle, but you were cursed with terrible friends.

But it's simply not true. The people who teach their audience to depend on friends and family are the worst. They are letting you down.

This book assumes that you have no social media following, friends or family to leave you reviews. If you can get a family member to leave an honest review after reading your book, that's great. But that is not where you should be directing your energy.

Reviews for Copies

People love free books, and there are several amazing platforms where you can post your book to find these people. This system is pretty simple. You post your book and say that you will give away a certain number of reviews. The only contingency is honest feedback from people after they have read your book.

Some of these systems are free, and some charge a listing fee. Depending on your budget you can work your way up the cost tree.

Book Country

This is a great platform to use before your book goes live. You can post early versions of your book and ask for readers and reviewers. This platform is built around helping writers with honest feedback. The more active you are in the community, the more reviews you can generate.

The platform offers to handle your book publishing for you, but don't waste your time with that. You already know how to do it on your own, so there's no reason to burn your hard-earned money.

Once you've gotten a load of reviews from the platform and are ready to launch, you can take your book down. You don't want a free version of your book competing with Amazon's paid version. When your book goes live, message your reviewers and ask them to copy and paste their reviews onto your book listing page.

LibraryThing

This website is a Goodreads alternative that isn't owned by Amazon (yet). It is a great place for authors and readers to connect. They have a wonderful contest program that they call Early Reviewers and Member Giveaway. You can run a contest and give away a few copies of your book to the winners. In your entry form, state that you would like a review in exchange for a free copy of the book.

They don't have to leave the review on Amazon to be a part of the program. Many people will leave reviews for your book on Library-Thing, Goodreads, social media and their blogs. All of these are wonderful, and you can use Amazon Author Central to add the best reviews to your listing page. You can also ask these excellent reviewers to copy and paste their review to Amazon.

The people on this site take their reviews very seriously, and they will give you fantastic feedback. If they find problems with your book and can't give it a positive review, they usually email you with a list of reasons they felt your writing was bad. It can be upsetting, but this feedback is solid gold.

If this happens to you with one of your books, assess the value of the critique. If they are on to something, take the time to update and improve your book. I like to run a giveaway here while my book is in pre-launch; this gives me time to fix any errors that come in and improve my book before it hits the general public.

NetGalley

NetGalley is a great platform where you can list a book for a short promotion. Usually, campaigns are run in groups of six books. You can find other authors running group promotions all the time. You pay around thirty bucks to have one of your books listed for a month.

People on NetGalley are all ranked based on their reviews. If someone tries to score a bunch of books without leaving reviews, their score drops and they are kicked off the platform.

The reviews you get from this platform are mixed in my experience. You will get a lot more traction here with fiction books than with non-fiction.

On my last campaign, I received the main review I used on that book's listing page. The lady left an eloquent and sophisticated review that warmed my heart. A later review compared me to a cult leader who eventually poisoned all of his followers with Kool-Aid; that review I chose not to share on my book listing page. You can't please everyone.

If you want to jump on a NetGalley promotion and want to find other authors to team up with, reply to one of my emails and I'll let you know. I'll also try to post some up-to-date links on where I find authors to team up with on my blog.

More Techniques

These techniques are just the tip of the iceberg, but they should be enough to get you started. As you will see when we plan out your launch, we want at least ten solid reviews before we run your book through the promotion cycle. Twenty reviews are even better, and completely achievable if you implement each of these techniques.

I have loads more methods for getting reviews that I share on my website. I'm always looking for new ways to connect with my readers and adapt to the changing online landscape. I continually test new methods to improve my book marketing, and once I confirm they work, I release them to my loyal customers and readers.

25

GENERATING HORDES OF TRAFFIC WITH KINDLE SELECT

Amazon does not want you selling books in other bookstores. To motivate you to choose exclusivity in your publishing, Amazon has put together several very powerful reward programs.

Kindle Select is the program you join when you promise not to sell your book on any other platform. This only includes the digital version. You can sell your paperback version anywhere you like. Since most other digital platforms represent less than ten percent of the market, it's worth staying exclusive with Amazon.

The first benefit of joining this program is Kindle Unlimited. This program often generates up to forty percent of my monthly revenue. It's a significant income boost. I use this program as a publisher and also a consumer. The program is perfect for me.

For the consumer, it's a monthly subscription service for $9.99 a month. It turns Amazon into a buffet. Instead of paying for every book you read, you simply pay that one monthly fee. You can hold up to ten books at a time on your Kindle, and as you finish them you can return books and grab new ones. As someone who reads thirty books a month, this program is perfect for me.

As a publisher, you can get paid for a customer that didn't pay you directly. Amazon tracks a massive budget every month for this program. The total purse is more than ten million dollars every month. They take the total income from Kindle Select customers to generate that purse value. Then Amazon calculates the total number of pages read across the platform. You get paid a percentage of the total purse based on your book page reads.

If that math sounds complicated, expect to get page $.005 per page read. That might not sound like much, but those numbers can add up. A one-hundred-page book will pay you fifty cents in royalties for a Kindle Unlimited read. If your book is 99 cents, you only get about thirty cents if the customer buys your book.

Many authors price their books high just to encourage readers to choose Kindle Unlimited. The platform used to pay on a different scale, but sneaky marketers were gaming the previous system. Writing longer books is now rewarded, and as someone who always shoots past his word count, I'm happy to be rewarded.

Promotional Days

As a member of Kindle Select, you can place your book on promotion five days out of every ninety. These promotional days are crucial to pushing your book up the rankings and getting noticed.

You can run a free day promotion or a countdown deal. A countdown deal puts your price onto a calendar and visitors can see that the price will soon rise again. You get a nice little timer on the page to create a sense of urgency. There are some advanced ways to use this type of promotion once your book is launched to rebuild momentum, but for the initial launch you will use the free promotion instead.

You can set up a day where your book will be free for twenty-four hours. It's very important to remember that all of Amazon runs on the Pacific Timezone. Never forget that or you will mess up some crucial timings with your promotions.

You don't have to use your days consecutively, and I never use all five in a cycle. For your initial launch promotion, you will use a promotion of 1-2 days and no more. If you run a five-day promotion, you burn up all your free days in one shot and your promotion will lose momentum. It's better to get ten thousand downloads in one day than two thousand downloads a day five times in a row.

Planning a Day

You want to wait until you have at least ten solid verified reviews on Amazon before you start planning a promotion day. I prefer to have at least twenty, but ten is workable.

Go into your Kindle dashboard and go to the promotions section. Choose your type of promotion and select a day from the little calendar that pops up. Once you click to confirm, your day is locked in.

Depending on your market, different days of the week might appeal to you. I think people base their favorite days to promote based on superstition. Some people swear by Tuesdays, and other will only run a promotion on Thursdays. I can't tell you the perfect day of the week because any day will work in my experience. I do prefer weekdays to weekends, but that's simply a personal preference.

The Announcement

Choose your promotion day at least a week in advance, but two is better if you can manage it.

Once you have your day selected there are dozens of websites that you need to notify. There are websites, newsletters, Facebook groups, and Twitter accounts all built around getting people deals on Kindle.

A customer will sign up for one of these platforms, and each day they will get notified about the best discounted books that day. Some groups want to know when books are on sale, and others only want to know about free books.

These sites come and go all the time. It's impossible to maintain an up-to-date list of the best places to announce your promotion. I will put a list on my website and try to update it continually, but you will always encounter new sites. If you run into one that isn't on my list, please feel free to email me about it.

There are two ways to let these sites know about your upcoming promotion. You can manually fill in the forms on each website. This process will take you about two to three hours. You can also get one of your kids or an assistant to do it.

The other option is to use a piece of software. There are a few solutions out there that do this, and each one works in a different way. Some of these tools are completely automated, and others just autofill the forms for you to speed up the process. I tend to use the slower tool because it does a better job of submitting, but it does cost $29 a promotion now. It used to be $15, but they raised their rates recently.

I think that's a little steep if I'm being honest. You will get more total downloads if you submit to sites manually, but I'll post links to the software options at ServeNoMaster.com/orbit.

For your first launch, every single download will count; I recommend you submit manually.

Turbocharge

For most of this process, I believe in saving every penny possible. I hope you appreciate that I've gone the extra mile to show you how to do each step for free. This entire process assumes that you have no following or social media presence.

The first promotion is how you kickstart your book out onto the world stage and start building your list. We have been saving as much money as possible because promotion day is the key to everything.

This is the one part of the cycle where I'll spend a load of money.

Some services charge a premium to tell their list your book is free. They cost anywhere from thirty to three hundred dollars, depending on how many eyeballs they can drive to your page.

If you have a marketing budget, this is where you want to spend it. I want to be totally transparent with you about each step in the book launch process. Every time I launch a book, I use a different set of services. Some services that were great six months ago burn out their lists by selling promotions to horrible books. I get on as many of their customer feeds as possible. I want to see what kind of books they are recommending to their audience.

As some services weaken, new ones pop up that are simply amazing. This fluctuation means you have to stay on the pulse of the Amazon game. If you visit my site, I'll keep you updated on what services I'm testing and the kind of results they generate.

Before you spend a penny, analyze if you even need to. If you have followed my system up to this point, posted your book cover on my Facebook wall and gotten the seal of approval from me, and then manually announced your promotional day to every site you find, you will generate around three to five thousand downloads on your promotional day.

For many categories, this is enough downloads to be number one. You only need to be number one in your category to launch your momentum.

If you are going after a tougher category like business books or fiction, then you will need to buy some traffic for your promotion. Some spaces are so competitive that you need huge numbers to generate enough momentum.

If you are launching a romance book, you need to go for the biggest traffic sources you can afford. Romance is so competitive on Amazon that you can get fifteen thousand downloads, and your book might not break the top one hundred.

Romance is a unique kettle of fish on Amazon, and requires a different long-term strategy. Romance is the most popular category on Amazon, but it also has the smallest number of subcategories. Last time I checked, there were around ten romance subcategories. You can sell one hundred paid units of your book in a single day and not even break the top 100 books in your category list.

For a super competitive niche, the best move is to make your first book free and then wait until you have a few more books in the series ready to start running promotions. That is when your books get profitable. You still want to run a very similar promotion; you just wait until you have the follow-up books to be revenue generators.

26

ANATOMY OF A LAUNCH

Nobody knows who you are. You are a zero in your new niche. You have no friends. But that's about to change if you follow this very simple formula.

I don't use a list to push my books up the ranking on Amazon. I use my books on Amazon to build my lists. This system allows me to break into any niche I want and establish a presence. It will do the same for you.

First, you are in pre-launch. During this phase you are writing and editing the book, generating the book cover and seeking out a few pre-launch reviews. Getting reviews at this point can be tough if your book is only done a week before you want to launch it.

Second, you go into top secret review phase. This is where your book is 99 cents, and you send out review copies to anyone who will take one. You don't announce your book to anyone yet. It's on Amazon, but you don't tell anyone about it. This phase is crucial because it is when you get verified reviews. A verified review means Amazon knows the person bought your book, and it is worth ten times the weight of an unverified review. You need at least ten, and preferably more than twenty, verified reviews before this phase is complete.

Third, you have your promotional day. The book will be free for 24-48 hours, and you focus on getting as much traffic as you possibly can. Buy as much traffic as you can afford and get the word out about your book. You want to get all of your ducks in a row before this promotion. All of your formats should be available and linked to one listing.

Fourth, when your promotion ends, put your book back at 99 cents for a day or two. Here's why. Some people on those free book lists won't notice your promotion until a day or two later. We miss emails all the time. Plenty of people will go check out your book. If it's back to $7.99 they will be disappointed they missed your chance and move on. The ones who have Kindle Unlimited might grab a copy if you're lucky.

If the same person comes to your book the day after a promotion and it's 99 cents, there is a good chance they will grab it. They missed the free day, but it's still on discount.

After a few days at 99 cents, it's time to bring your book up to full price. This is when your book starts making your money, and it's properly launched. If you followed each step in this process, then your book will maintain that momentum. To keep the sales coming in, you need a continual flow of reviews.

We already handled that by setting up your last page and email appeals. This infrastructure will keep your book generating revenue for a very long time.

Before You Upload

Before you upload your book to Amazon, you want to make sure all your ducks are in a row. Put as much time and energy into perfecting your writing as you can. If you can afford an editor, it will be worth it in the long run. I will post updated links to editors I find with reasonable prices and turnaround times.

You want your book to be as close to perfect as possible before you send it out into the world. If you can, generate some pre-release reviews so that your book can hit the ground running.

Review Phase

For two weeks, getting reviews is your full-time job. If you don't take this phase seriously, all of your other work will have been for nothing. As customers, we all have a threshold for the number of reviews a book needs to have before we take it seriously.

Nobody wants to buy a book with a single review on it; we simply don't trust it.

If your book followed my entire method and is any good at all, you will be able to get enough reviews to get your book out there. Put in the effort now and you will be rewarded with long-term revenue and powerful sales numbers.

Free Days

Your free day is when you show Amazon that you can bring external traffic. You are establishing that you take your book seriously and that you are Amazon's partner. The site appreciates people who generate their own traffic, and rewards them.

Make sure you get as much traffic as you need to dominate your categories during this promotion. This effort will pay for itself as soon as you switch to back to paid.

Back to Paid

Leaving your book discounted for a few days will help to carry over that free day momentum into the paid rankings. For every category, Amazon has two sets of top one hundred books. There are the paid top one hundred and the free top one hundred.

Having a few 99-cent days will bridge the gap between these two lists for you.

Maintain the Momentum

The key to maintaining momentum is setting up your structures correctly. Setting up your email system to encourage people to leave in-depth reviews will make a big difference.

The game does not end the moment you upload your book to Amazon; that is only the beginning. As new books enter the market, they will attempt to steal your market share. Amazon tests new listing styles all the time and will frequently change how your page appears.

Tend your book listing like a garden to ensure that it grows revenue for you every month. Be active in the cultivation of your rankings. When your book has a drop-off, you will need to do a big review push and then a free day promotion to get back up there.

Depending on how your book is doing, you may need to run a promotion every few months or once a year. These secondary promotions don't require the same intensity as your first one. Just appeal for reviews, make the book free for a day and then announce to all the free sites. You usually don't need to buy any traffic for follow-up promotions.

27

HOW TO MAKE TEN TIMES
MORE MONEY

W e talked at the very start about building a business. Now it's time to magnify your income exponentially. This section is where we turn you from an independent author to indecently wealthy.

Some authors are unaware of the universe outside of Amazon, and if that includes you, please allow me to open your eyes. Books on Amazon are the bottom of the market. I come from the direct response world, and the first book I wrote in that market sells for $47, and it sells loads of copies every single day. People will pay a LOT more for the same content outside of Amazon. Once you launch your book on Amazon, building an external infrastructure will allow you to sell more expensive items and generate a lot more revenue.

You can sell loads of amazing things to your audience every single day. As long as you provide your new list with lots of value, they will be glad to stick with you for the long haul.

For every dollar you make within Amazon, your list should generate another ten dollars in net revenue for you. If you are making ten dollars a day on royalties, this chapter will put another zero in there and get you to a hundred bucks.

Build a Tribe

The mailing list is how you cultivate and grow your tribe. A tribe is more than just a following or a fanbase. A tribe is something that is powerful and wonderful. If you can build a tribe of just 1,000 people, you are set for life and will never have to work again.

A tribe is a group of people that follow you and are part of the journey for a long time. Serve No Master is my brand, and it's the message of my tribe. It's about helping people to open up revenue streams and giving them total control of their destiny. This book is just one method to achieving that path.

When you publish your first book and it actually works, you are going to turn from a reader into a member of my tribe. Nothing turns people into believers like making them money. I have total faith in my system, and I know that if you take action, you will see remarkable results.

I want people to be a part of my tribe for years, not months. I want to help you build your entire business over the next two decades. I want to be there as you launch book one and book twenty, as you build a giant brand and then sell it and sail off into the sunset.

Building a tribe is about taking the long view. Giving your people as much value as possible and rewarding their loyalty with success. I have some more advanced Kindle courses. I sell a private coaching course that's pretty expensive. But there aren't links to those anywhere in this book. I might eventually mention them to you in an email, but that won't be for a while.

I would much rather you launch your first book, make a little money and then use that money to invest in my more advanced material. I believe in funding your training from profits, not debt.

I get several emails a week from people who want my advanced training and want to put it on a credit card or borrow money from a family member. If that is your situation, I will not accept your money. I will not put anyone in a financially precarious position.

I teach several methods of making money fast that don't require any investment. You can follow this system and get your first book onto Amazon without spending a penny. If you have Kindle Unlimited, you might have even read this book for free. That's great! I have no problem with that because Amazon still pays me.

On my site, I teach a method for writing blog posts as a ghost writer that pays up to $100 an hour. You can raise enough capital in six weeks to fund anything you want. If you can't afford it, please don't buy another course from me.

You bought this book, and that makes you a part of my tribe. It's my responsibility to take care of you before I take care of myself. I already live on a tropical island in paradise. My life is taken care of. Let's focus on you first.

This is the tribe mindset, and you should have it with your followers in any space. Let your desire for their good fortune always come first.

Sell More Books

The best thing to do with your list and growing tribe is selling more books. There are two ways to do this. The first way is to ask your tribe to share your book on social media and post reviews.

I just got an email today that was AWESOME. This great dude wrote me a long email about how inspired he was by Serve No Master. He was so excited that he drew an awesome picture of a robot waving around a copy of the book. It was so cool.

I emailed him back and asked him to post his email as a review to Amazon and to include that picture. I want everyone to see it. When was the last time you saw a book review that included a picture of a robot waving around the book? His enthusiasm in that review will increase my page conversion. More people will buy the book when they read his review.

Then those people will get excited, and soon I will have loads of pictures of robots and unicorns and goblins holding copies of my book in the reviews.

The second way to sell more books is to let your readers know about the other books you've written. All the people who joined my list when they read Serve No Master have no idea that this book exists. When they read that book, I hadn't written it yet. If they visited my author page, they only saw a single book.

Now that this book is live, I emailed all of them to let them know about this book, and a lot of them grabbed a copy. It was a nice boost to my ranking and helped to get me some early momentum. (At least I hope that's what happens. I'm writing this before I upload the book, obviously.)

Your list should get follow-up emails about your other related books to let them know your offers. "Did you enjoy my book on push-ups? I have a great book on squats that you're going to love..."

Many people will be glad to find out about your other books that are relevant to them. When you send someone back to Amazon, you can get paid twice for the same sale.

Get Paid Twice

Amazon has an affiliate program. They pay you every time you send someone a recommendation. The program starts at a 4% commission and grows up to 8% if you send enough people each month. You might think that that's peanuts, but bear with me.

If you sell your book for $2.99, your royalty is around two bucks. If you send customers through your affiliate link, Amazon will pay you an additional twelve cents. That seems like small potatoes until you apply volume. If you sell ten books a day through recommendations, that's an extra dollar a day, and I'm just getting started.

Amazon will give you 4% of everything that person buys for the next twenty-four hours. If your reader buys your book you make twelve cents, but if they purchase a TV a few hours later, you could earn a commission of over $100. That's pretty cool.

You get paid twice for selling your book. You get the royalty for being the author and a little bump for being the affiliate.

You can then recommend other stuff on Amazon that is relevant to your space. If your audience suffers from tinnitus, noise-canceling headphones might help. If they are struggling with baldness, a great hat recommendation can go a long way. If you are teaching people about yoga, they need to get their yoga mats and pants somewhere.

You know that your audience likes to buy stuff from Amazon because they already bought your book there. Recommending other cool stuff that will benefit them is a natural and profitable progression.

Sell Direct

When you sell products directly from your website, you can charge much higher price points. You don't have to share the money, and you can turn a few pennies into some serious money.

Let's imagine that you wrote an awesome yoga book. You run a small studio in your town, but you want to reach that wider audience. Your book is doing pretty well. You sell ten copies a day at $2.99 and walk away with $20 profit. That's an extra $600 a month in income. It's not enough to let you retire from teaching classes eight hours a day, but it's a start.

Here's how I'm going to make you rich. You get some of your students to help you out. You set up professional lights and borrow some cameras for the day and record your own enhanced yoga DVDs. You have video content to offer your readers which gives them increased value.

You can sell your videos for $17 each on your website. You can even sell a package of three hour-long sessions for $29. That's a pretty good deal. Three videos for less than two would cost on their own. Because you are in charge of your operation, you deliver the videos as direct downloads. Your customers don't have to wait a week for a DVD to show up, and you don't have to pay shipping costs.

After processing fees, you'll make around $16 profit from each sale of your single video. A single video sale is worth EIGHT times more than a single book sale. When you get people to transition from your book, you make a lot more money.

If you convert just one buyer from your book to grabbing a yoga video from you each day, your income jumps from $600 up to $1,080.

That number is not quite accurate. You have your customer's email information. You can send yoga tips and blog posts. You get multiple touches with your customers. You get multiple chances to sell your video, so you can expect around thirty percent of your book customers to buy a video eventually.

That pushes your income to over $2,000 a month. Just by offering something more valuable at a reasonable price point directly from your website. Removing Amazon from the equation allows you to triple your income with one extra day of work.

We're closer to that ten to one income ratio, but not quite yet.

Designing a Free Gift

The free gift is where many new authors hit the wall. I see a lot of new authors who go out and buy some garbage PLR written by a non-native speaker and throw a few box shots into their book to sell it.

That's not cool at all.

I'm going to open the kimono here. Once I decided on the free gift for this book I spent AGES on the image design. I spent hours messing around with the images to get them exactly how I want. High-quality images convey value and effort. The effort is real because I spent a long time working on the image myself.

If possible, your free gift should be worth more than your Kindle book. Give away music, an audiobook version of your content, a short story, a printable version, or anything else you can think of.

The challenge with the free gift is that it's unique to each niche and offer. Take a look at what the people around you are offering, and beat them. That's my primary approach to marketing in general. I can't give you one-size-fits-all advice because that's so disingenuous. Romance readers want a different gift than people buying cookbooks.

If you are struggling to come up with a gift, reply to one of my emails, and I'll help you come up with something awesome. I usually try to find a way to magnify the value of the book in some way. This book teaches you how to make money selling books on Amazon, and using audiobooks to boost your income from the same work is an excellent value on top of that. You will increase your income 30% if you let me email you. That's a pretty good trade-off.

The key is to give your readers as much value as possible.

The Mechanics

The technical process starts with setting up your emailing software. This software is often called an autoresponder. The two main products I like are called Aweber and GetResponse. I have affiliate links to each service on my website. If you sign up through one of my links, I would be super grateful, and I will be glad to help you if you get stuck in the technical part of the process.

Once you have chosen your software, create an opt-in form using their provided HTML tool. I know it sounds scary, but it takes thirty seconds. It creates a box where people can enter their email address and a button they click to submit. You put this little form on a page all by itself on your website.

Like at the start of this book, you create a link on the first page of your book that takes people to that page. Kindle will automatically load a web browser that takes them to your page. When set up correctly, your reader can fill in their email address, hit send and then click the X to close the page and be back reading your book in under five seconds.

Your software then captures that email address and starts sending a series of automatic emails. The first message is a thank-you message that includes their free gift. The following messages are designed to strengthen the relationship and eventually magnify your income.

Emails for Dollars

I promised that I would increase your income tenfold, and here is where I'm going to do it. Selling your own stuff is cool and selling stuff on Amazon is nice, but it takes time to make products and Amazon only pays 4% to new affiliates.

Let's continue with our yoga example:

You have a book teaching people the basics of yoga. Once someone reads that book, there are several other ways you can give them value. You can help them find a great local school by analyzing reviews and generating a recommendation for them. You can also point them to your favorite yoga DVDs on Amazon. You can even recommend great yoga pants or a yoga mat. There are many directions you can take your audience.

When you recommend something on Amazon, you get a commission from Amazon of 4-8%. If you sell a video for $19.99, Amazon will pay you from forty to eighty cents for that recommendation. It's not much, but it's better than nothing.

Looking at the direct response market, my favorite platform is called Clickbank. They have a program called Yoga Burn. You can find links to their sales page at ServeNoMaster.com/orbit. (On that page, I have a ton of follow-up information and links to all the things discussed in this book. Sometimes you just need a visual, and I have loads of bonus material on that page.)

The Yoga Burn program is a series of DVDs that sells for $37. If you recommend that series to your book readers, Clickbank will pay you 75%. You can earn nearly $28 for each recommendation. This product costs double the Amazon DVD price but pays out thirty-five times more money. Which offer would you want to promote?

When you mix in high-quality affiliate offers with your own content, you magnify your income.

Most direct response products have an entire upsell sequence behind them. You recommend that first product for $37, and when people buy it, they immediately see another product for $77. Many of those sales turn into more than three hundred dollars.

Sending a single customer to a great product can generate you an extra two hundred bucks from just ONE customer.

Cultivating Your List

You have dollar signs in your eyes right now, and it's my fault for putting them there. Please listen to this warning. Do not recommend stuff to your audience that will not improve their lives. Do not recommend things you don't use or believe in just because they offer a great commission.

As you build your list, you will face greater and greater temptation. When you can make ten grand promoting something, maintaining integrity gets pretty hard. If you don't prepare in advance, the temptation will overwhelm you.

Your list will turn off and tune out boring newsletters. Think about your experience as a customer. Which emails do you open and which ones do you ignore? If I sent you an email every day with something to buy, you would unsubscribe in a few days. Nobody wants to be treated like an ATM.

Whenever you are thinking about an email to send out, remember to always give them value first. When your primary focus becomes income, you risk alienating more and more of your fanbase. You'll notice that my emails are filled with additional content to take you beyond this book. This book is double the length I intended. But it still only covers ten percent of what I know about Amazon.

I have podcast episodes and blog posts where I can share more advanced techniques and provide visual walkthroughs of these processes. My goal is to build engagement with you and give as much value as possible. Build your list with the exact same mindset. These are people who trust you, and you must honor that trust by guiding them down the right path.

Your initial goal is to open as many lines of communication as possible. Right now we are having a one-way conversation. I'm talking, and you are listening. That's not a conversation. Get your audience to connect with your social media presence, to listen to your podcast and to comment on your blog posts. The more people interact with your content, the more likely they are to take action.

Give as much value as you can on each of your platforms and

develop strong relationships with your readers. The stronger the connection, the more powerful your list will become.

Some marketers have a list of over one hundred thousand email addresses, but less than three percent of their list opens any given email. That's the same as building a list of three thousand people that open every email you send. Focus on quality and you will build a powerful business fast.

28

KEEP THE SALES ROLLING IN FOR YEARS

Amazon is a fickle beast. Authors who work hand-in-hand with Amazon to generate sales and growth get the most attention. Their books appear in more promotions and on select lists all the time. Amazon can list your book in many special locations. The site has all the power, and you must be active to maintain momentum.

Authors who become complacent and stop managing their profiles will slowly fade into oblivion.

Following the method you just learned, you can successfully launch your books. Some of your books will hang in the top twenty listings for an entire year before they slip. Others will only hang for a few months.

Once your book is live, there will be other authors coming after you. They will launch their books to try and knock off your crown. If you want to stay at the top of the mountain, you must actively fight for position.

Remember your three key metrics. Amazon only cares about traffic, sales, and reviews. You should continually refine your review-gathering process. Always seek ways to get more reviews and to turn more of your active readers into reviewers. Add incentives to your emails for people who leave reviews. Encourage them to take action even weeks after they read your book.

As long as you maintain engagement, you can strengthen the relationship. Some people who didn't feel like leaving a review right after reading your book might feel ready after a few weeks of additional content. That relationship-building will turn more and more of your readers into reviewers.

More Content

The Internet is a hungry monster. As a ravenous monster, this beast demands more and more content. Your biggest fans will rip through your content faster than you can believe. On my first blog, I had over one thousand posts. When a new fan would get excited, they would consume everything in three days or less.

When I get turned onto a new podcast, I tear through their back catalog very quickly. I can get through two hundred episodes in a week or two.

Your biggest fans are the ones who want the most content.

When the book is published, the writing is not complete. You must provide continual content through your blog, social media and emails. If you have a podcast, you must deliver content like clockwork.

Right now I put out five podcast episodes a week, but it's not nearly enough content for my fans. I need to up my game and generate more blog posts to stay ahead of my followers' desires. The more blog posts I write, the more they will consume.

All of these people are looking for content to read and share with their friends. It's hard to "give away the gold," and many writers turn stingy with their content. That's just not my mindset. I don't need to hide my best material behind a paywall. The people who love me the most will buy stuff either way.

If you feed the beast properly, you turn your traffic into a cycle. You launch your first book following the Breaking Orbit method. Your first readers form the core of your new list. As you engage them, you move them from reading emails to your social media profile. Over time they start to share you with their friends. They post and tweet and like and mention your blog posts and books and videos. All of this engagement brings you new fans. You then send these new fans to your book.

These brand new fans found you through social media, not Amazon. They read your book and become members of your tribe. They become so excited that they post about you on their social media profiles, and soon their extended network is buying your book and joining your tribe. This is how you turn your book launch into a self-perpetuating cycle. Keep generating content and the machine keeps spinning.

When the Book Drops

You're going to have good and bad days. If the book next to you spends a thousand bucks on traffic one day, that book is going to sell more units than you.

When you notice your ranking and sales numbers slipping, wait a few days before panicking. One of my books is always number two or three in its category. Once, the book slipped down to number six, and I worried that the book was dead. A few days later, Amazon course-corrected and I was back to number two.

If your book slips below the top 30,000, then you need to take action. Set up a free promotion and launch a new traffic push. Amazon always wants to see new reviews on your page. A few months after your launch, you can reuse all of the review sources I shared above. Their audience will have changed, and you will find a whole new batch of reviewers.

During that free promotion day, get as much traffic and momentum as you can. Share with your list and get them to share with all their friends. The skeptics who were interested in your book, but not willing to buy it, will gladly read it for free. They will then become engaged, join your tribe, and leave awesome reviews.

29

PULL THE TRIGGER

You've done it! We're at the end of the book. My journey is coming to an end, but yours is just starting.

This is where we separate the readers from the doers. If you read this book out of curiosity and have no desire to ever write a book, that's cool. I appreciate you taking the time to read my story.

This chapter is for everyone else. If you want to succeed, you have to take action. You have all of the steps you need in this book. There are additional walkthroughs on my blog, and advanced lessons on my podcast. You can email me with any questions, and post to my Facebook page when you want feedback. You have knowledge, tools, and support to get you through writing and launching your first book.

The first step is planning your book. You might not have an idea yet, and that's ok. Start searching around the Kindle categories until you find something that appeals to you. Analyze the keywords and categories for profit and opportunity. When you find that good fit, study the competition.

Looking at the competition will give you a target word count. Take that word count and divide it into manageable pieces. If you can write five hundred words a day, you can set a deadline to finish your first draft.

Write Your Book

Nothing will happen until you start putting words on a page. This action step is crucial. Whether you write by hand, use Scrivener, or dictate your book, do whatever it takes to get those words written.

The idea phase is pleasant, but the writing stage is where reality is created. Put in the time, get your head down and write that book. Release the creativity that is within you. You know the same deep research method that I use for my work. You have every single piece of knowledge you need to write something fantastic.

Writer's block will never enter your life because you know how to research and create a flawless outline. Writing is my favorite part of the process. It's so exciting. Each word you create brings you one step closer to immortality.

Launch Your Book

When your writing is complete, it's time to edit and then launch your book. Ignore any thoughts or negative words from your friends. They will try to stop you from launching.

I waited two years between writing and launching my first book. I was afraid to release it into the universe and wanted to wait until the time was just right. I was a fool, and my hesitation cost me thousands of dollars. Learn from my mistake.

I launched Serve No Master forty-one days ago. Here I am writing the conclusion to the next book in the series. I'm a big believer in speed to market. The faster you can create and launch books, the sooner you will have the momentum you need to quit the job you despise. To pay off those credit card debts. To serve no master.

Join My Tribe

Thank you so much for reading Breaking Orbit. I want you to break the gravitational chains that have limited your income for so long.

I have tons more material to help you along your journey and to support you as an author and as an entrepreneur.

Please check out my blog and give my podcast a listen. They are loaded with free content to help fill in the gaps in your knowledge. I'm always adding new content, and I want nothing more than to get that email from you bragging about your new bestseller or paying off that final credit card. Those moments are the ones that change me and make all of my effort worthwhile.

You may have felt like something was missing from this book and that I didn't go into deep enough detail on something. Please check out the Breaking Orbit page on my site to see if it's in the extended material. If you don't find what you're looking for, please email me. You don't have to write a bad review because something you wanted wasn't in here. I'd much rather get your feedback directly and improve this book to better meet your needs.

I respond to every email personally, and I do update and improve my books as things change. I want my material to be as valuable as possible. This book is not an altar to my hubris. It is not about ego or fame. I desperately want to help you achieve the same life that I live. I am sitting here on the beach at sunrise on my paradise island.

My dreams came true. Now it's your turn. Let me help you. Let me show you the path—so that you too can achieve it.

Serve. No. Master.

ONE LAST CHANCE

I believe in second chances. Now that you've read this entire book, you know that I have a whole series of bonuses waiting for you on the other side. Just click the link below and enter your email address; I will immediately send you my guide to boosting your income with audiobooks. It's so easy that it will blow your mind.

After that you can expect a few more emails with all of the additional content I mentioned during the course of this book. I will include some of my top secret advanced training, several custom paperback templates, and even more top secret book review strategies.

Turbocharge your results NOW.

ServeNoMaster.com/audio

MORE INFORMATION

Throughout this book I mentioned other books, images, links, and additional content. All of that can be found at:

https://servenomaster.com/orbit/

You don't have to worry about trying to remember any other links or the names of anything mentioned in this book. Just enjoy the journey and focus on taking control of your destiny.

FOUND A TYPO?

While every effort goes into ensuring that this book is flawless, it is inevitable that a mistake or two will slip through the cracks.

If you find an error of any kind in this book, please let me know by visiting:

ServeNoMaster.com/typos

I appreciate you taking the time to notify me. This ensures that future readers never have to experience that awful typo. You are making the world a better place.

ABOUT THE AUTHOR

Born in Los Angeles, raised in Nashville, educated in London, Jonathan Green has spent years wandering the globe as his own boss – but it didn't come without a price. Like most people, he struggled through years of working in a vast, unfeeling bureaucracy.

After the backstabbing and gossip of the university system threw him out of his job, he was devastated – stranded far away from home without a paycheck coming in. Despite having to hang on to survival with his fingernails, he didn't just survive; he thrived.

Today, he says that getting fired with no safety net was the best thing that ever happened to him. Despite the stress, it gave him an opportunity to rebuild and redesign his life.

One year after being on the edge of financial ruin, Jonathan had replaced his job, working as a six-figure SEO consultant. With his Rolodex overflowing with local businesses and their demands getting higher and higher, he knew that he had to take his hands off the wheel.

That's one of the big takeaways from his experience. Lifestyle design can't just be about a job replacing income, because often, you're replicating the stress and misery that comes with that lifestyle too!

Thanks to smart planning and personal discipline, he started from scratch again, with a focus on repeatable, passive income that created lifestyle freedom. He was more successful than he could have possibly expected. He traveled the world, helped friends and family, and moved to an island in the South Pacific.

Now, he's devoted himself to breaking down every hurdle entrepreneurs face at every stage of their progress, from developing mental strength and resilience in the depths of depression and anxiety, to developing financial and business literacy, to building a concrete plan to escape the 9-to-5, all the way down to the nitty-gritty details of teaching what you need to build a business of your own.

In a digital world packed with "experts," there are few people with the experience to tell you how things really work, why they work and what actually works in the online business world.

Jonathan doesn't just have the experience; he has it in a variety of spaces. A bestselling author, a "ghostwriter to the gurus" who commands sky-high rates due to his ability to deliver captivating work in a hurry, and a video producer who helps small businesses share their skills with their communities.

He's also the founder of the Serve No Master podcast, a weekly show focused on financial independence, networking with the world's most influential people, writing epic stuff online and traveling the world for cheap.

Altogether, it makes him one of the most captivating and accomplished people in the lifestyle design world, sharing the best of what he knows with total transparency, as part of a mission to free regular people from the 9-to-5 and live on their own terms.

Learn from his successes and failures and Serve No Master.

Find out more about Jonathan at:
ServeNoMaster.com

BOOKS BY JONATHAN GREEN

Non-Fiction

Serve No Master Series

Serve No Master

Serve No Master (French)

Breaking Orbit

20K a Day

Control Your Fate

BREAKTHROUGH (coming soon)

Habit of Success Series

PROCRASTINATION

Influence and Persuasion

Overcome Depression

Stop Worrying and Anxiety

Love Yourself

Conquer Stress

Law of Attraction

Mindfulness and Meditation Ultimate Guide

Meditation Techniques for Beginners

Social Anxiety and Shyness Ultimate Guide

Coloring Depression Away with Adult Coloring Books

Don't be Quiet

Develop Good Habits with S.J. Scott

How to Quit Your Smoking Habit

The Weight Loss Habit

Seven Secrets

Seven Networking Secrets for Jobseekers

Biographies

The Fate of my Father

Complex Adult Coloring Books

The Dinosaur Adult Coloring Book

The Dog Adult Coloring Book

The Celtic Adult Coloring Book

The Outer Space Adult Coloring Book

Irreverent Coloring Books

Dragons Are Bastards

Fiction

Gunpowder and Magic

The Outlier (As Drake Blackstone)

ONE LAST THING

Reviews are the lifeblood of any book on Amazon and especially for the independent author. If you would click five stars on your Kindle device or visit this special link at your convenience, that will ensure that I can continue to produce more books. A quick rating or review helps me to support my family and I deeply appreciate it.

Without stars and reviews, you would never have found this book. Please take just thirty seconds of your time to support an independent author by leaving a rating.

Thank you so much!

To leave a review go to ->

https://servenomaster.com/orbitreview

Sincerely,
Jonathan Green
ServeNoMaster.com

Made in the USA
Columbia, SC
06 November 2019